Men-at-Arms • 544

Italian Colonial Units

1882–1960

Gabriele Esposito • Illustrated by Giuseppe Rava

Series editors Martin Windrow & Nick Reynolds

OSPREY PUBLISHING
Bloomsbury Publishing Plc
Kemp House, Chawley Park, Cumnor Hill, Oxford OX2 9PH, UK
29 Earlsfort Terrace, Dublin 2, Ireland
1385 Broadway, 5th Floor, New York, NY 10018, USA
E-mail: info@ospreypublishing.com
www.ospreypublishing.com

OSPREY is a trademark of Osprey Publishing Ltd

First published in Great Britain in 2022

A catalogue record for this book is available from the British Library

ISBN: PB: 9781472851260; eBook: 9781472851291;
ePDF: 9781472851284; XML: 9781472851277

22 23 24 25 26   10 9 8 7 6 5 4 3 2 1

Editor: Martin Windrow
Index by Richard Munro
Typeset by PDQ Digital Media Solutions, Bungay, UK
Printed in India by Replika Press Private Ltd

MIX
Paper from
responsible sources
FSC® C016779
www.fsc.org

Osprey Publishing supports the Woodland Trust, the UK's leading woodland
conservation charity.

To find out more about our authors and books, visit
www.ospreypublishing.com . Here you will find extracts, author interviews,
details of forthcoming events, and the option to sign up for our newsletter .

Dedication

To my parents Maria Rosaria and Benedetto, for sharing with me the heritage of
my family deriving from the Italian colonial period; and also, to the memory of all
the brave soldiers who died far from their homeland while serving in
Italy's colonies.

Acknowledgements

Thanks are due, as always, to the series editor Martin Windrow, for his support
and advice. Another special acknowledgement goes to Giuseppe Rava, for his
brilliant colour plates recreating some fascinating but almost forgotten
military units.
All the photos reproduced in this book have been generously provided to the
author by Gabriele Zorzetto, a leading expert on the history of Italy's colonial
troops, who has collected a large amount of precious material and has
published several excellent books on the subject – see Select Bibliography.
The original images of the maps of East Africa and Libya, respectively, may be
found at (https://upload.wikimedia.org/wikipedia/commons/a/aa/Italian_East_
Africa_%281938%E2%80%931941%29.svg). and (https://commons.wikimedia.
org/wiki/File:Map_of_traditional_provinces_of_Libye-en.svg).

TITLE PAGE

Artist's impression of Eritrean *ascari* fighting Mahdist cavalry on the Eritrean-
Sudanese border in 1890. The officer on the left is wearing the M1887 khaki
tropical uniform, as issued to the *Cacciatori d'Africa* in 1889. His men wear their
second uniform, introduced from 1890: a red *tarbusc*, and simple white jackets
and trousers set off by a coloured waist-sash. At the decisive Second Battle of
Agordat, 2 December 1893, Col Giuseppe Arimondi's victorious force numbered
some 2,300 Eritreans of the 2nd, 3rd and 4th *Battaglione fanteria indigena* and a
cavalry squadron, led by about 75 Italians.

ITALIAN COLONIAL UNITS
1882–1960

BACKGROUND

A veteran *sciumbasci* (roughly, sergeant-major) of the Libyan Division organized in 1935, which fought in Ethiopia before being dispersed again in 1937. Although the pouch-bandolier was normally mounted-troops' issue, his red *tachia* cap displays the infantry branch badge of a brass crown, bugle-horn and crossed rifles, below three silver rank stars. The black cloth triangular brassards temporarily attached over the upper sleeves of his pale khaki jacket show red rank chevrons, and re-enlistment stars indicating his length of service.

The Kingdom of Italy was only unified as a single nation under King Victor Emmanuel II of the royal house of Savoy in March 1861, and the complex historical process known as the *Risorgimento* was only finally completed in September 1870.[1] Early Italian governments struggled both to instil a sense of cohesive national identity in a historically divided country, and to find a suitable diplomatic stance towards the great European powers of the day. In search of both a patriotic cause and international status, they believed that Italy – although a late-comer – should join the 'scramble for Africa' in competition with Britain, France, Portugal, Spain, and more recently Belgium and Germany.

In this ambition Italy was handicapped by internal difficulties. Despite having a large population in an extensive territory, it was a poor country: millions of Italians, especially in the south and Sicily, had a high birth-rate but insufficient employment to support them. Italian society was still largely rural, and it lacked social cohesion, since the wealthy ruling classes tended to respond harshly to the discontents of the impoverished masses. Consequently, during 1870-1910 up to 9 million of the rural poor had no choice but to cross the Atlantic in search of better lives – and this mass emigration to the Americas further damaged the national economy. Upon the death in 1878 of Victor Emmanuel II he was succeeded by his son Umberto. This admirer of Prussian militarism pursued a harshly conservative agenda, and, rather than addressing the many problems within his nation, King Umberto I looked outwards.

Italian governments started to look around in search of African or Asiatic territories that might be colonised. During the last years of Victor Emmanuel's reign the Italian Army had been completely reformed and notably expanded, and now seemed to be ready for deployment overseas to gain territories and glory for its young nation. By 1880 most of Africa had already been colonised, mainly by Britain, France and Portugal, with just a few regions remaining theoretically open to Italian penetration. Initially Italy sought a potential possession located not too far from Sicily, since its main goal was to settle large numbers of Italians from the poorest southern areas in a nearby colony. Tunisia was

---

1   See MAAs 512 and 520, *Armies of the Italian Wars of Unification 1848–70 (1)* and *(2)*.

an obvious choice, but in 1881 the French imposed a protectorate over that country without even considering Italian diplomatic requests, and at the same time Britain did the same in Egypt.

Eritrea and Somalia

Consequently, in 1882 the Italian government turned its attention to the Red Sea, where there were some coastal areas that had not yet been occupied by other powers. North-eastern Africa had been dominated for centuries by the Abyssinian empire (modern Ethiopia). Unusually, this state had some degree of political centralization, could muster large military forces at need, and showed little fear of European expansionism. Being a vast territory inhabited by warlike tribes, Abyssinia was not considered as a desirable colonial acquisition by the older European powers. (During 1867–68, for example, Britain had conducted a punitive expedition there, but had withdrawn after achieving tactical victories, preferring to support a new and more pliable ruler.)

To the north and east of Abyssinia, however, lay two distinct areas on the western and south-western shores of the Red Sea, facing Ottoman-ruled Arabia. Eritrea, facing Yemen, had been ceded by the Ottomans to Egypt in 1865, while Somalia, further south-east below the Gulf of Aden, was fragmented into a number of native states. Neither region had great natural resources, but after the opening of the Suez Canal in 1869 their location astride the international trade route to India and beyond made them strategically attractive. In 1882, after quietly establishing that Egypt had no great interest in the region, the Italians decided to initiate a cautious colonisation of Eritrea.

This was followed by Somalia in 1889, after both France (1883) and Britain (1884) had also created their own colonies on the adjoining coastline. The Italians progressively occupied much of Somalia after a series of negotiations with local native rulers and with the Sultanate of

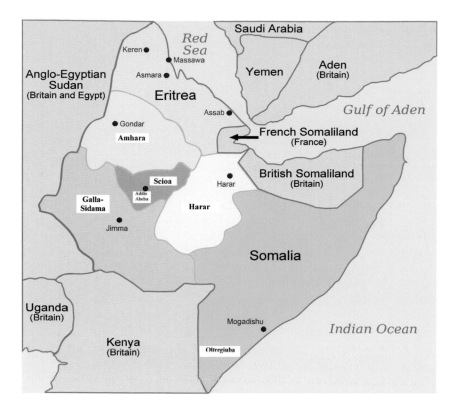

Italian East Africa in 1940. (Original map modified by Wikimedia user 'Themightyquill', CC BY-SA 3.0)

Eritrean cavalry instructors from the *Squadrone Indigeni ('Penne di Falco')* in Tripoli, Libya, in 1912. The new military units organized by the Italians in Libya were mostly trained by experienced Eritrean soldiers who were sent to North Africa. These three instructors are wearing the M1908 khaki two-pocket jacket for cavalry; note the two frontal pleats, just visible starting below the shoulder-strap buttons. It is worn over the traditional long white blouse and loose white trousers, with an entirely red waist-sash. For the colours of the *tarbusc* wrapping, see Plate A3; the brass badge shows a crown above a circle on two crossed lances.

Zanzibar, which exerted a kind of protectorate over a good part of the region. Neither Eritrea nor Somalia proved to be particularly lucrative for Italy, since they lacked all infrastructure and their terrain was unsuited to agriculture, so they attracted only a very limited number of Italian settlers. At the end of the 19th century the Italians tried to expand further inland by attacking the Abyssinian empire, but this advance ended in shocking failure when an Italian army was destroyed by the Abyssinians at the battle of Adowa (1896). This caused public outrage in Italy, whose rulers recognized that there were no more lands to conquer in the Horn of Africa.[2]

Libya

The years that followed saw much civil unrest in Italy, and the military suppression of bread riots in Milan in May 1898 eventually provoked the assassination of King Umberto I on 29 July 1900. A decade later King Victor Emmanuel III's government once again sought overseas distractions. By 1911, Libya

---

2   See MAA 471, *Armies of the Adowa Campaign 1896: The Italian Disaster in Ethiopia.*

was the last African province of the Ottoman Empire, held by only a weak Turkish garrison. When it became apparent that the Ottoman state was on the verge of crumbling under the attacks of the new Balkan nations, the Italians decided to invade Libya before it could be colonised by any other power. The Italian-Turkish War of 1911–12 saw a series of Italian victories over the Ottomans in the coastal areas; but when the war ended Italian troops were left in control of this coastal fringe alone, while the vast desert interior was still in the hands of stubbornly defiant local tribes. It took the Italians until the early 1930s to finally pacify the whole territory (at a high cost in casualties), and, since Libya's great natural resources had yet to be discovered, all they got for their investment was a huge 'sand-box' with some agricultural settlements along the coast.[3] Despite previously close relations with Germany and Austro-Hungary, Italy entered World War I on the Entente (Allied) side in May 1915, which provoked Turkish military support for the Libyan rebels.

Colonisation under Fascism

The rise to power of Benito Mussolini's National Fascist Party in 1922 would have a great impact on Italy's colonial policy, since *Il Duce* sought to transform his country into a resurrected 'Roman Empire'.

During World War I most of Italy's Libyan territory had been re-taken by local rebels, inspired by the Senussi religious movement and aided by Turkish agents. Probes inland to recover lost ground began in 1919–21, but from 1922 Italian forces in Libya were greatly reinforced (including by

---

3   See MAA 534, *Armies of the Italian–Turkish War: Conquest of Libya 1911–1912*, and MAA 466, *Armies of the Balkan Wars 1912-13.*

The three Libyan governorates in 1930. (Original map modified by Wikimedia user 'Bourrichon', CC BY-SA 3.0)

Somali infantrymen presenting arms to a reviewing officer in 1928. They still wear the white version of the M1906 uniform that was adopted for parade dress from 1913. The white waistcoat with red edging and embroidery identifies these soldiers as serving in the 3rd Native Company; for other colours, see under Plate C1.

colonial native troops), and supported by armour and aircraft. Generals Badoglio and Graziani employed harsh methods to suppress the tribes; in 1931 the army in the Sahara reached the far south of Fezzan, and the Cyrenaican resistance leader Omar Mukhtar was captured and executed. The following year Libya was declared pacified, and in 1934 the separate governorates of Tripolitania, Cyrenaica and Fezzan were unified as a single colony. During the 1920s–30s Italian settlement and exploitation of the coastal region increased considerably.

NCOs of the mounted Eritrean *zaptiè* in 1936, wearing the white parade version of the M1928 uniform. The gendarmes are distinguishable by the white-metal *Carabinieri* flaming-grenade badge on the *tarbusc*, below rank stars and above a specialty badge. The waist-sash in entirely red. The Italian authorities considered the Eritrean gendarmes to be their best African soldiers.

In October 1935, Mussolini launched a new invasion of Abyssinia (Ethiopia). Italy transported the equivalent of about 13 Army and Fascist Militia (MVSN) divisions to East Africa, and, with superior modern equipment, was able to crush organized Ethiopian resistance in less than a year. In 1936 Eritrea and Somalia were assembled with the newly-defeated Ethiopia into *Africa Orientale Italiana* (Italian East Africa). For a brief period the Kingdom of Italy had thus acquired an African empire, but local resistance continued in southern and western Ethiopia.

World War II

In June 1940, Italy entered World War II on Germany's side, but its only practical supply route to Italian East Africa passed through the British-controlled Suez Canal. In August the Italians briefly expelled the garrison of British Somaliland. In September they attacked British-occupied Egypt from Libya, but failed spectacularly. They were forced to appeal for German help, and thereafter Gen Rommel's Afrika Korps quickly became the dominant Axis force in North Africa. British forces captured Italian East Africa in spring-summer 1941, as the Ethiopian population rose against their occupiers alongside the British counter-invasion. Two years later, despite Rommel's several victories in the meantime, Anglo-US forces finally defeated the Axis in Tunisia in May 1943, capturing the last Italian troops in Africa (although see Chronology, under 1950–55).

A *capo* (sergeant) of the Somalian *Dubat*, 1936, wearing an off-white turban and wrap-around skirt *(futa)*, with the red tasselled cord distinctive of his rank (see under Plate C3). Note the metal whistle hanging below his belt, for passing simple orders at a distance.

An Italian officer with Libyan *Spahi* photographed in a desert camp in 1940. By the outbreak of World War II the Libyan light cavalrymen had partly abandoned their traditional uniform illustrated as Plate F3, replacing the dark blue *burnous* cloak with a more practical khaki jacket of the kind used by the *Savari*. The badge worn on the front of the *tachia* showed two crossed lances and bugle-horns.

CHRONOLOGY

North-East Africa:

15 November 1869   Italian ship-owner Raffaele Rubattino purchases Bay of Assab, Eritrea, to instal commercial facilities.

10 March 1882   Italian government purchases Rubattino's concession.

1884   Entrepreneur Vincenzo Filonardi becomes Italian consul to Sultanate of Zanzibar, and negotiates commercial concessions in Somalia.

5 February 1885   Italy occupies city of Massawa on Eritrean coast. During 1885 Italy signs first treaty with Sultanate of Zanzibar, aiming to create protectorates in Somalia.

25 January 1887   About 15,000 Abyssinian warriors, led by warlord (Ras) Alula, attack Italian border fort at Saati, Eritrea, but *c.*1,200 mainly locally-recruited *ascari* soldiers, with two guns, repulse heavy assaults.

26 January 1887:   **Battle of Dogali.** 500-man Italian relief force for Saati under LtCol De Cristoforis is ambushed on the march by Ras Alula with *c.*7,000 men, later heavily reinforced; column overrun, 430 Italians killed. Saati abandoned soon afterwards.

October 1887   New Italian expeditionary force of *c.*20,000 troops shipped to Eritrea to complete its conquest, while Abyssinia is distracted by internal war.

1 February 1888   Italians re-occupy Saati. Abyssinian emperor (Negus) John IV mobilizes forces and moves on Eritrea, but in early April withdraws without attacking.

8 February 1889   Sultanate of Obbia, component native state of Somalia, becomes Italian government protectorate. (Filonardi will be appointed governor.)

March 1889   Negus John IV fatally wounded in battle against Sudanese Mahdists; he names Ras Mangascià of Tigré as his heir, but Menelik of Shewa seizes throne.

7 April 1889   Somalian Sultanate of Migiurtinia also accepts Italian protectorate.

2 May 1889   Treaty of Uccialli (Wuchale) between Italy and Abyssinian empire. It suits Menelik II to co-operate temporarily with the Italians against Ras Mangascià in the northern province of Tigré, but Italian misinterpretation of other terms of treaty will cause friction.

26 July 1889   Italians occupy Cheren (Keren) in Eritrea.

3 August 1889   Italians occupy Asmara, future capital of Eritrea.

1 January 1890   Italian territories on Red Sea are officially unified as new colony of Eritrea; although this is tolerated by Menelik II, he continues playing the Italians off against his local rivals.

March 1890   Menelik II receives submission of chiefs led by Ras Mangascià and Ras Alula.

27 June 1890   First Battle of Agordat. Italian force repulses Sudanese Mahdist incursion into Eritrea.

1 November 1891   Gen Oreste Baratieri is appointed Italian C-in-C in Eritrea.

12 August 1892   Treaty between Italy and Sultanate of Zanzibar; Italy gains control of important Somali ports, including Mogadishu, initially for 25 years.

21 December 1893:   **Second Battle of Agordat.** Col Arimondi's force of 2,300 defeats *c.*10,000 Sudanese; Emir Ahmed Ali and *c.*1,000 of his warriors are killed.

16 July 1894   Italians take Cassala, eastern Sudan, from Mahdists.

January 1895   Italian troops advance into Abyssinia's northern province of Tigré.

12 January 1895:   **Battle of Coatit.** Gen Baratieri's 3,800 Italian-led *ascaris* defeat 15,000-plus Tigréans led by Ras Mangascià; casualties 324 vs *c.*4,500.

March 1895   Italian forces continue advance into Tigré, taking towns of Adigrat, Aksum and Macallè (Mekele).

17 September 1895   Negus Menelik II orders general mobilization.

9 October 1895   Italians defeat Ras Mangascià at Debra Ailà.

1 December 1895   Menelik II leads national forces to support Ras Mangascià in Tigré.

7 December 1895:   **Battle of Amba Alagi.** Some 30,000 warriors, led by Ras Mangascià and Ras Mekonnen of Harar, destroy Maj Toselli's 2,350-strong column, killing 2,000-plus Italian troops.

20 December 1895   Abyssinians besiege small Italian garrison at Macallè.

21 January 1896   Survivors of Macallè garrison surrender their weapons in exchange for their lives.

1 March 1896:   **Battle of Adowa.** After the defeat of Amba Alagi, Gen Baratieri's army in Tigré face a choice: either retreat towards Eritrea with huge Abyssinian forces in close pursuit; or regroup for a pitched battle. The 14,500 well-equipped Italians and *ascaris*, with 56 guns, face up to 100,000 warriors (more than half of them with breech-loading single-shot rifles). Logistic pressures on both sides argue for a pitched battle, and Baratieri's staff persuade him to take the gamble. On the night of 29 February, the Italians advance with difficulty in three separate brigades, with a fourth in reserve. Dawn finds the tired units dispersed over several miles of broken, unfamiliar terrain. The disoriented brigades are attacked and destroyed piecemeal, including the reserve. The routed and fleeing survivors are closely pursued and hunted down, the main groups crossing the Belesa river to safety during 3–4 March. This worst of any defeat yet suffered by a white colonial army reportedly costs Baratieri about 6,133 killed, 1,428 wounded, and 3,000-4,000 captured – 10,000-plus casualties, mostly Italians – and all his artillery. Abyssinian casualties may total up to 17,000.[4]

26 October 1896	By Treaty of Addis Ababa, Italy renounces any claim on Abyssinian territory and withdraws from Tigré, and Abyssinia recognizes Italian possession of Eritrea.
25 December 1897	Cassala in Sudan is ceded by Italy to Britain.
(2 September 1898	Gen Kitchener's Anglo-Egyptian army destroys Mahdist army at battle of Omdurman in Sudan.)
29 July 1900	King Umberto I is shot by anarchist assassin, and succeeded by his son King Victor Emanuel III (r. 1900–1947).
1906	Sultanate of Zanzibar recognizes Italian protectorates of Obbia and Migiurtinia in Somalia.
5 April 1908	Italian possessions and protectorates in Somalia formally unified into single colony.

Libya:

29 September 1911	Outbreak of Italian-Turkish War.
2 October 1911	Threatened by Italian Navy, Turkish garrison of Tripoli retreats inland.
4 October 1911	Italian Navy bombards and occupies port of Tobruk.
5 October 1911	Italian Navy lands sailors to occupy Tripoli.
11–19 October 1911	Italian Army troops landed at Tripoli, Derna, Homs and Benghazi, all occupied at little cost but remaining isolated.
23 October 1911	Costly repulse of major Turkish and Libyan attack at Sciara Sciatt oasis outside Tripoli.
5 November 1911	Strong Italian reinforcements landed in Tripoli. On same day, Italian parliament announces annexation of Tripolitania and Cyrenaica (western and eastern provinces, respectively.)

8 July 1912	Italians occupy Misrata, last Ottoman-held port in Libya.
18 July 1912	Italian torpedo boats threaten Ottoman defences in Turkey's Dardanelles straits.
18 October 1912	Treaty of Lausanne brings Italian-Turkish War to an end, with cession of Tripolitania and Cyrenaica to Italy.
19 July 1913	Italy declares occupation of Somalia complete.
World War I: by July 1915	Libyan insurgents recapture entire Italian territory apart from coastal towns protected by Navy. Major Senussi, Tuareg and other *bedouin* revolts follow in French Algeria and British Egypt.
in April 1917	Britain and (briefly) Italy reach terms with Senussi, but local Libyan revolts continue.
Interwar: 1919-21	Italian Army carries out series of offensives against Libyan insurgents.
1922-24:	Reinforcements sent by Mussolini's new Fascist government recapture Tripolitania and parts of Cyrenaica.
15 July 1924	Colony of Somalia enlarged with southern Oltregiuba region ceded by Britain.
1925-32	By methods including use of aerial gas-bombing and mass internments, Italians finally pacify remainder of Libya.
1 January & 3 December 1934	Tripolitania and Cyrenaica, and finally Fezzan, are united into colony of Libya.

Ethiopia (former Abyssinia):

27 December 1934	Mussolini orders mobilization in Eritrea and Somalia.
3 October 1935	Italian invasion of Ethiopia; Negus Hailé Selassié declares war.
28 November 1935	Marshal Badoglio replaces Gen De Bono as C-in-C East Africa.
November–December 1935	Steady Italian advances on both northern (Eritrean) and southern (Somalian) fronts.
4–16 December	Ethiopian victory at Dembeguina Pass, Tigré.
12–20 January 1936	At Genale Dorya on southern front, Gen Graziani, with air support, defeats Ethiopian advance.
20–24 January 1936	Italians halt Ethiopian 'Christmas offensive' on northern front in Tembien area.
31 March 1936	Badoglio defeats Ethiopian main army at Maychew (Mai Ceu) in Tigré.
5 May 1936	Italian troops enter capital, Addis Ababa.
9 May 1936	Mussolini proclaims birth of Italian Empire, unifying Ethiopia, Eritrea and Somalia as Italian East Africa.

---

4   See MAA 471, *Armies of the Adowa Campaign 1896: The Italian Disaster in Ethiopia*.
This record of colonial disaster would stand until the loss of some 13,200 of Gen Silvestre's Spanish troops at the fall of and during the retreat from Anual, in the Rif highlands of NE Morocco, in July–August 1921.

World War II and after:			
10 June 1940	Italy enters World War II on Germany's side.	**8 November 1942**	Anglo-US Operation 'Torch' landings in French North Africa.
4–17 August 1940	Italian forces in East Africa occupy British Somaliland.	**November 1942-May 1943**	Tunisian campaign; final Axis surrender in Tunis on 11 May.
13 Sepember1940	Italians from Libya invade Western Desert of British-held Egypt.	**10 July–17 August 1943**	Allied conquest of Sicily. Mussolini deposed on 25 July, and regime
9 December 1940	Gen O'Connor's British offensive captures Italian forward positions.		under Marshal Badoglio seeks armistice with Allies.
6 February 1941	Rapid British advance takes Benghazi.	**8 September 1943**	Italian armistice announced; Allied landings in Italy begin the next day.
January-May 1941	British and Ethiopian forces capture Italian East Africa; Mogadishu falls on 25 February, and Keren on 27 March. Hailé Selassié re-enters Addis Ababa on 5 May.	**10 February 1947**	By Treaty of Paris, Italy cedes its colonial possessions. Libya is placed under joint Anglo-French occupation until becoming independent in 1951, and Eritrea is annexed to independent Ethiopia.
28 November 1941	Fall of Gondar, last Italian enclave, though colonial troops will continue guerrilla activity.	**21 November 1949**	United Nations assigns Somalia to temporary Italian control, as the Trust Territory of Somaliland.
February-November 1942	Large Italian forces in North Africa continue to fight the British, but are in practice secondary to Gen Rommel's more mobile and better-equipped German Afrika Korps.	**1950–55**	Italian military mission raises new Somali units.
November 1942-January 1943	After British victory at El Alamein, Axis troops retreat across Libya.	**1 July 1960**	Italian and British Somaliland are united as independent Republic of Somalia.

THE UNITS: ERITREA

1885–95:

Italian and native infantry

The first Italian troops only reached the Bay of Assab in 1885, three years after its acquisition by the government. They consisted of small detachments from units of the metropolitan *Regio Esercito* ('Royal Army'): 6th Company,1st *Bersaglieri* (light infantry) Regiment; 10th Co, 4th *Bersaglieri* Regt; 2nd Co, 7th *Bersaglieri* Regt; 12th Co, 8th *Bersaglieri* Regt; 1st Co, 17th Fortress Artillery Regt; sapper platoon; detachment *Carabinieri Reali*.

In a challenging climate, amid an unfamiliar tribal population, their numbers proved inadequate for controlling the surrounding territory. Consequently, on 30 April 1885 it was decided to employ local soldiers. The Italians recruited from among irregulars who had previously served the Ottoman and Egyptian garrisons, traditionally termed *basci buzuk* (literally 'crazy heads', but in practice 'auxiliaries'). The first two 100-man companies were commanded by Hassan Agah Osman, an Albanian officer of the former Egyptian garrison. Ill-disciplined, and unreliable for serious combat, the irregulars were still useful for holding small outposts and keeping order among the tribal population.

From late in 1885 these irregulars were expanded and restructured into two battalions known as *orde*. Each 500-strong *orda* was commanded by a *sangiak,* and organized in five *tabur* or companies. Each *tabur,* commanded by a *bimbasci,* comprised four 25-man *buluk* platoons, each led by a *bulukbasci*. One of the two units was the *Orda Interna,* tasked with garrisoning the urban settlements as a sort of gendarmerie, and the other was the *Orda Esterna,* to perform proper military functions in the hinterland. The *Orda Interna* continued to exist until 31 March 1891,

ABOVE LEFT
NCO and soldiers of the Eritrean 5th Native Infantry Bn 'Ameglio' photographed in Tripoli, 1912. For this campaign the previously disbanded 5th Bn was re-formed with companies from the 1st-4th Battalions. They are wearing M1904 white jackets, with standing collars and two breast pockets, over their white blouses and trousers. The tassel of the red *tarbusc* and the waist-sash are in five mixed colours – black, red, green, blue and yellow – giving the sash a sort of 'tartan' effect.

ABOVE RIGHT
Eritrean soldiers of the temporary *Squadrone Cammellieri* that was sent to Libya in 1912. Here they wear their parade dress of white turban, blouse and trousers; on campaign, a khaki jacket with two breast pockets was worn over the blouse. In Libyan units rank was indicated by red points-up chevrons applied to the sleeves, rather than the looped-on black brassards employed in Eritrean and later Somali units.

when its members were reorganized into four independent platoons: three 'garrison' and one 'customs guard'. However, poor performance led to the disbandment of the *Orda Esterna* on 28 September 1888, though its best elements were absorbed into newly-raised regular Eritrean infantry units.

In May 1888, following the defeat at Dogali in 1887, the new Italian commander Gen Baldissera had decided to form regular native units that he intended should be better trained and disciplined than the *basci buzuk*. These men were called *ascari* (a Turkish term for 'soldiers', already used in East Africa). Originally eight battalions of Eritrean infantry were planned, but a shortage of recruits limited them to four *battaglioni di fanteria indigena*. These 'battalions of native infantry' at first had five companies each, soon reduced to four. Each of these was structured in two half-companies, with six platoons (increased to eight in time of war). For a brief period during June 1889–September 1890 the four Eritrean battalions were assembled into a single *Reggimento di Fanteria Indigena*, but they soon reverted to the more flexible and practical structure of independent battalions.

Simultaneously, the Rome government – recognizing the Abyssinian threat to the colony – also decided to raise a new Italian military corps to serve overseas: the *Cacciatori d'Africa*. These 'African Chasseurs' were supposed to permanently replace the *Regio Esercito* detachments previously sent to serve in Eritrea. The first two regiments were officially formed on 14 July 1887, with picked volunteers from the metropolitan army; the 1st Regt comprised two battalions of *Cacciatori* and one of *Bersaglieri*, while the 2nd had three of *Cacciatori*, each battalion having four companies. In addition, a single 150-man squadron of *Cacciatori a Cavallo* was recruited from the best elements of the metropolitan cavalry, but to serve as mounted infantry. (After this arrived in Eritrea a temporary 1st Sqn of African Cavalry made up from metropolitan detachments, which had been sent out six months previously, was disbanded in June 1888.)

During that year, despite these new formations, the government was also obliged to send a large number of Italian metropolitan units to Eritrea to stabilize the situation. This *Corpo Speciale d'Africa* had the following order of battle:

I Brigade: 1st & 2nd Regts *Cacciatori d'Africa*; 3rd Battery, African Mountain Artillery

II Bde: 1st & 4th Regts African Infantry;1st Bty, African Mtn Arty

III Bde: 1st Regt, African *Bersaglieri*; 1st Bn, African *Alpini* (mountain infantry); 2nd Bty, African Mtn Arty

IV Bde: 2nd & 3rd Regts African Infantry; 1st Co, 17th Fortress Arty Regt

(plus) Two batteries of Field Arty, two companies of artillery train, and three of sappers.

It is important to note that all these so-called 'African' units were simply temporary assemblies of metropolitan detachments, and only the *Cacciatori d'Africa* could be defined as truly 'colonial'. Following the Treaty of Uccialli, the *Cacciatori a Cavallo* were disbanded in the spring of 1890, and on 11 December 1892 the *Cacciatori d'Africa* were reduced to a single battalion with six companies; this would be disbanded in 1919.

Supporting arms

This reduction of the white colonial force coincided with the progressive expansion of the native troops, which was both economically and politically beneficial. On 5 October 1888 the authorities raised the first Eritrean *Plotone di Cavalleria Indigena*; this 'cavalry' platoon had just 30 troopers, mounted on mules or dromedary camels to act as mounted infantry. In October 1889 this was enlarged to become the horse-mounted 160-man *Squadrone Esploratori Indigeni* ('Squadron of Native Scouts'), led, like all native units, by Italian officers and NCOs. Employed to protect the colony's submitted tribes from cattle-rustlers and Abyssinian border-raiders, the Eritrean troopers soon proved to be excellent fighters. In November 1890 they were expanded to two squadrons: the existing one was redesignated the *Squadrone di Cavalleria Indigena 'Asmara'*, and the new one the *Squadrone di Cavalleria Indigena 'Cheren'*. Each squadron had four platoons, of which three had horses and one had mules; in addition, the 'Cheren' Sqn also had a small detachment mounted on dromedaries for desert patrols. Both squadrons of Eritrean cavalry did well against the Mahdist incursions; nevertheless, in April 1894, to cut costs, the 'Asmara' Sqn was disbanded and the 'Cheren' Sqn lost its camel platoon. The Eritrean cavalrymen were known as *Penne di Falco*, because they wore a hawk feather on their headgear.

During 1888–89 the Italians also organized a *Batteria Indigeni da Montagna*, initially consisting of 60 Italians (mostly officers or NCOs) and 100 Eritreans. On 28 May 1891 it was restructured as two four-gun batteries. In November 1893 a new *Compagnia di Cannonieri Indigeni* was also formed to garrison the coastal fortifications at Massawa. In April 1894 the second mountain battery was disbanded, again for economic reasons.

Eritrean *bulukbasci* (sergeant) of the 8th Libyan Native Bn, 1917. This unit was one of three from Cyrenaica that had to fill the vacancies in their ranks by incorporating two companies of Eritrean *ascari*. This soldier is wearing a khaki M1908 jacket over the universal white blouse; the tassel of the *tarbusc* and the waist-sash of his unit are in two colours, red and black. The ranks in native infantry units were *ascaro* (private), *muntaz* (corporal), *bulukbasci* (sergeant) and *sciumbasci* (roughly equivalent to the Italian *sergente maggiore* or *maresciallo*).

Eritrean *zaptiè* in 1921; they all wear the khaki M1908 jacket except the NCO crouching right, who has the white parade version. All these gendarmes wear the red *tarbusc* with a blue tassel and white-metal flaming-grenade badge. Note the additional silver braid on the collar, and the entirely red waist-sash, which were typical of *zaptiè*. Two men, at top centre, have added red decorative *aiguillettes* to their uniforms, as often seen on special occasions.

An Eritrean *sciumbasci* (sergeant-major) in the 19th Mixed Bn, photographed in Tripolitania during 1925. This was clearly taken on some unusual occasion: as well as his regulation *tarbusc* and khaki M1908 jacket, he is wearing a white waist-sash and some sort of tribal 'kilt', and carrying not only an M1891 Carcano cavalry carbine but also a straight *kaskara* broadsword and a hippo-skin shield.

1895–1935:

Native infantry

In 1895, before the outbreak of the new conflict with the Abyssinian empire, the Eritrean *Truppe Indigene* were rapidly expanded. The infantry were increased to eight Native Battalions each named after its commanding officer, as follows: 1st 'Turitto', 2nd 'Hidalgo', 3rd 'Galliano', 4th 'Toselli', 5th 'Ameglio', 6th 'Cossù', 7th 'Valli' and 8th 'Gamerra'.

At Adowa, on 1 March 1896, the 1st, 6th, 7th and 8th Native Inf Bns formed Gen Albertone's Native Bde, with 1st Native Mtn Bty, while 3rd Native Inf Bn was attached to Gen Ellena's reserve 3rd Brigade. Each battalion had about 950 riflemen, and the battery four 75mm guns; in total, some 2,000 *ascari* were killed.

In March 1902, after the removal of the Abyssinian threat, the 5th-8th Bns were disbanded, but this lull did not last long. Several companies from Eritrean Native Bns were employed against local rebels in Somalia during 1897–1908, and in 1912 the Eritrean forces were fully mobilized to support Italy's invasion of Libya. The *ascari* were far superior to European troops in desert terrain and climate, especially in Fezzan, Each of the four battalions had to provide one company in order to form a new, initially temporary 5th Battalion. The *ascari* performed with distinction in Libya, and consequently the total establishment was re-expanded to eight battalions during 1912. Four additional battalions were raised during

1913, but it soon became clear that these 12 units had exhausted the resources of Eritrean manpower. From 1914 new battalions would have to be recruited largely from neighbouring territories – Sudan, Ethiopia and Zanzibar – to meet the threat posed by the Senussi uprising in Libya.

The conditions of service offered were attractive by contemporary African standards, and it did not prove difficult to recruit new *ascari*. These units were numbered in sequence following the 12 'true' Eritrean battalions, but because they drew upon diverse manpower they were designated *Battaglioni Eritrei Misti* ('Eritrean Mixed Battalions'). By 1927 a total of 14 such units were raised, permanently stationed in Tripolitania and Cyrenaica.

Between 1912 and 1935 the following 'Eritrean' battalions were active; note that 'dbd' = disbanded, 'ref' = 're-formed', and 'rsd' = 'raised':

Native Battalions:

1st N Bn 'Turitto'; 2nd N Bn 'Hidalgo'; 3rd N Bn 'Galliano'; 4th N Bn 'Toselli'; 5th N Bn 'Ameglio'; 6th N Bn 'Cossù' (dbd 1928, ref 1935); 7th N Bn 'Valli' (dbd 1925, ref 1935); 8th N Bn 'Gamerra' (dbd 1927, ref 1935); 9th N Bn 'Guastoni' (dbd 1928, ref 1935);10th N Bn (dbd 1928, ref 1935); 11th N Bn (dbd 1925, ref 1935); 12th N Bn (dbd 1925, ref 1935)

Mixed Battalions:

13th M Bn (rsd 1914); 14th M Bn (rsd 1914); 15th M Bn (rsd 1914, dbd 1933, ref 1935); 16th M Bn (rsd 1916, dbd 1933, ref 1935); 17th M Bn (rsd 1916); 18th M Bn (rsd 1916, dbd 1934, ref 1935); 19th M Bn (rsd 1918); 20th M Bn (rsd 1921, dbd 1930, ref 1935); 21st M Bn (rsd 1925, dbd 1930, ref 1935); 22nd M Bn (rsd 1926); 23rd Md Bn (rsd 1927, dbd 1928, ref 1935); 24th M Bn (rsd 1927, dbd 1928, ref 1935); 25th M Bn (rsd 1925, dbd 1928, ref 1935); 26th M Bn (rsd 1925, dbd 1929, ref 1935).

The pattern visible here shows that of the 12 'true' Eritrean Native battalions, only the first 5 were retained after the pacification of Libya; the other 7 were all disbanded during 1925–28, and re-raised only in 1935 on the eve of Mussolini's invasion of Ethiopia. Of the 14 Mixed battalions raised during and after World War I, only 5 were retained continuously after the end of the Libyan campaigns; the others were disbanded during 1928–33, but re-raised in 1935. The government intended to commit large numbers of native troops to Ethiopia, and transferred all the Eritrean Native and Mixed battalions stationed in Libya to East Africa during the mobilization of 1935.

Supporting arms

In October 1896 the single *Squadrone di Cavalleria Indigena 'Cheren'* was reorganized into two horsed half-squadrons and one camel platoon; on 17 June 1902 it was redesignated as simply the *Squadrone Indigeni*. Reduced over time to just 100 men, it was returned to an establishment of 200 during the 1935 mobilization. Meanwhile,

Eritrean *ascari* of an unidentified battalion photographed during a parade in Rome, 1930. They are wearing the universal white blouse, which remained in use after 1928 only for very special occasions. They wear an entirely red waist-sash and have added red *aiguillettes* to their right shoulders; note also the rifle badge on the *tarbusc*, and the unusual ammunition bandoliers.

on 28 February 1899, the single camel platoon had been disbanded, but during the Libyan campaign in 1912 the Italians formed an Eritrean *Squadrone Cammellieri* to counter the desert rebels. This unit was short-lived, however, since its mounts, accustomed to the rocky terrain of their homeland, found the deep, soft sand of North Africa difficult.

In 1895 a second Eritrean mountain battery was raised, and both took part in the Adowa campaign. After the 1st Mtn Bty's heavy losses in that battle the two batteries were consolidated into a single unit with four sections. During the same emergency, fearing Abyssinian attacks on their coastal settlements, the Italians raised a second *Compagnia di Cannonieri Indigeni* in Asmara, but these two garrison artillery companies were soon amalgamated. During 1898-1902 the 2nd Mtn Arty Bty was temporarily re-formed, becoming permanent in 1912. During 1913 both mountain batteries contributed to the formation of a 3rd, and the *Compagnia di Cannonieri Indigeni* was redivided into two independent companies. In 1917 a 3rd Co of Garrison Arty and a 4th Bty of Mtn Arty were formed; the former was disbanded in 1922 and the latter in 1926.

Minor units

On 30 September 1898 the Italians organized an independent 400-strong *Compagnia Costiera*, which was tasked with patrolling the Eritrean coastline in small detachments. In 1906 this was redesignated the *Compagnia Confinaria*, and transferred to the western border of Eritrea to counter Abyssinian raiders; it was disbanded in 1909. In 1917 the *Compagnia Costiera* was re-raised, and survived until 1929. In 1908, reliable Eritrean *ascari* were used to form an independent *Compagnia Amhara* to garrison Mogadishu in Somalia, which survived until 1926. From 1912, some dozens of Eritrean soldiers of various branches of service were detached to Libya as instructors for the local colonial troops then under organization; being Arabic-speaking Muslims, they proved particularly useful in this role. During 1913, following the deployment of many Eritrean units to Libya, the authorities raised a new garrison company in the capital, Asmara. In 1915 this *Compagnia Presidiaria di Asmara* was

Eritrean *'Penne di Falco'* in 1935; the troopers are all wearing the new khaki uniform introduced in 1928, and display the usual *tarbusc* decorations of the Eritrean cavalry. At the beginning of the war with Ethiopia in 1935 there was only one Group of Squadrons operational, but by 1937 another four such units had been organized.

transformed into a depot company, tasked with training new recruits for the Eritrean infantry units. During several changes of title, this company retained its functions until 1935.

In 1930, after most Eritrean battalions had left Libya, two Eritrean garrison companies were organized there: the Presidial Company of Derna, and the Presidial Company of Fezzan (both disbanded in 1937). In 1931, five short-lived *centurie* (companies) of Eritreans were created in Libya to escort the first Italian convoys sent to Kufra oasis in the Sahara.

1935: Italian officers in tropical dress supervise training by Eritrean artillerymen serving 75/13 howitzers. The gun crews wear the M1928 khaki uniform, with the artillery's black cap tassels and yellow waist-sashes.

Specialist units

In 1887 three companies of engineers were raised in Eritrea, reduced to two in 1891 and to one in 1898. In 1899 the remaining *Compagnia del Genio d'Africa* was reorganized into one section of telegraphists and three of sappers. Disbanded in 1902, it was re-formed in 1911, and in 1920 was expanded into one *Compagnia Specialisti* (engineers) and one *Compagnia Zappatori* (sappers). In 1928 these were amalgamated into a single *Compagnia Mista* ('Mixed Company'), and a second was formed in 1935. The Eritrean engineers had some motor vehicles from 1915, but a single *Sezione Automobilisti* was organized only in 1923; this became autonomous from the engineers for a brief period in 1931–32, before being re-absorbed.

During 1887, the Italians also raised three companies of the train (logistic troops) in Eritrea; these were reduced to one in 1891, which was temporarily disbanded in 1898. During the following decades the train corps of the Eritrean colonial forces changed designation several times; it was progressively reduced to just 40 men, before finally being disbanded in the early 1930s.

In May 1910 the first two experimental machine-gun sections were created in the Eritrean forces; each of these comprised an Italian officer, an Italian NCO and 18 *ascari*. The experiment was successful, and, over time, was expanded; by 1922 each company in the Eritrean infantry battalions had its own machine-gun section. In 1929 the four MG sections of each battalion were grouped into a single platoon attached to the 4th Company.

Eritrean radio-telegraphists of an engineer *compagnia mista* in the mid-1930s. They wear the M1928 khaki uniform, with the distinctive purple cap-tassel and waist-sash of the engineer branch. The lower badge on the *tarbusc* shows the engineers' elaborate crossed axes under a flaming grenade.

Paramilitaries and auxiliaries

Soon after their arrival in Eritrea the Italians began to organize a form of local police corps. These Eritrean gendarmes (called *zaptiè* – again, a Turkish term in use in Egypt) were tasked with patrolling the colony's main settlements and keeping order in the markets. On 15 October 1888 the *zaptiè* were structured as two 25-man platoons; these were grouped with the single company of *Carabinieri Reali* that had been sent to Eritrea, to form a new *Compagnia CC. RR. dell'Eritrea* ('Royal Carabinieri Company of Eritrea'). Over time the number of *zaptiè* was increased to 150; between 1918 and 1930 they were redesignated the *Corpo di Polizia* , but then reverted to the previous title. These highly trusted native gendarmes were also employed as military police to prevent desertion from Eritrean units, and they bore the same ranks as the soldiers.

The *Guardia di Finanza*, Italy's militarized Customs Guard, recruited 35 auxiliary *basci buzuk* soon after its arrival in Eritrea; in 1891 these were absorbed into a new independent unit known as *Buluk Doganieri*. In 1932 this became a new 50-man *Corpo delle Guardie Doganali*.

In 1894, following the expansion of its Eritrean possessions, the Italian government decided to organize a local *Milizia Mobile,* from time-expired *ascari* who were still fit enough for static garrison duties, and who could be mobilized in emergencies, in return for tax exemptions. When mustered for the first time in summer 1894 it numbered four companies (soon increased to eight), and after the disaster of Adowa a complete 'reserve battalion' was temporarily mobilized. In 1898 the Mobile Militia was structured in 12 companies, which could be assembled into groups of four to raise three temporary battalions (from 1903, two) in case of need. This successful new organization later provided cadres for the new regular infantry battalions formed from 1912.

In addition to the regular *Milizia Mobile,* from 1897 the colonial authorities also organized the *Chitet*, an irregular levy to operate in the Eritrean countryside. This was raised from among the male inhabitants to perform auxiliary duties in case of military emergencies. In 1909 the *Chitet* was transformed into the *Riserva*, and received a more stable organization based on companies; these, in case of mobilization, could be grouped to raise six reserve battalions. In emergencies, the colonial authorities could thus form a total of eight temporary second-line battalions.

In addition to all these, the authorities in Eritrea could also call at need upon the so-called *Bande Irregolari* ('Irregular Bands') – contingents of irregulars provided by allied Eritrean tribal warlords. Strong alliances with local chieftains who led large feudal retinues had been negotiated since the Italians' first arrival in Eritrea. In 1889 they recognized 16 so-called *Bande Assoldate* ('Recruited Bands') totalling some 1,400 warriors. In 1892, after the expansion of Italian territory, the existing bands were divided into three main categories: *Bande in servizio permanente*, which served on a regular basis and were equipped by the Italians; *Bande in servizio ausiliario,* which were more autonomous, and were not supplied; and *Bande in congedo,* a last reserve of older warriors. However, the Adowa campaign demonstrated that these bands were of little military value, and in 1903 they were discontinued.

Complete disbandment of auxiliary corps would have caused local revolts, so the Italians did retain eight *Bande Armate* to serve as a sort of rural police. 'On paper' only, in case of war these could have been supported by another eight irregular *Bande di Guerra.* In 1930 the *Bande Armate* were organized into three Groups corresponding to the three major geographical regions of Eritrea: Highland Group (three bands, in the north of the colony); Eastern Lowland Group (two bands, in the south-east); and Western Lowland Group (four bands, in the south-west). In addition, there were two autonomous bands in the isolated region of Dancalia.

1935–36:

Maximum expansion

In 1935, during Italian mobilization for the invasion of Ethiopia, the colonial forces of Eritrea were greatly expanded and reorganized. The ten infantry battalions existing in 1934 were expanded to 26, of which 20 took part in the invasion. The 4th Mtn Arty Bty, disbanded in 1926, was re-formed in 1935, and all three batteries were expanded into artillery groups (roughly, battalions). Two entire divisions were formed with Eritrean soldiers, grouped into a *Corpo d'Armata Eritreo* commanded by Gen Alessandro Pirzio Biroli, as follows:

Eritrean Army Corps

I Eritrean Division	*II Eritrean Division*
I Brigade	**II Bde**
I Group of Eritrean Bns:	III Group of Eritrean Bns:
1st, 6th & 16th Native Bns	5th & 21st Native Bns
V Group of Eritrean Bns:	VII Group of Eritrean Bns:
7th & 15th Native Bns	4th, 19th & 22nd Native Bns
I Group of Eritrean Mtn Arty	III Group of Eritrean Mtn Arty
III Bde	**IV Bde**
II Group of Eritrean Bns:	IV Group of Eritrean Bns:
3rd & 11th Native Bns	9th, 12th & 17th Native Bns
VI Group of Eritrean Bns:	VIII Group of Eritrean Bns:
2nd, 13th & 24th Native Bns	8th & 20th Native Bns
III Group of Eritrean Mtn Arty	IV Group of Eritrean Mtn Arty

The single cavalry squadron of 1934 was expanded into the *Gruppo Squadroni di Cavalleria Coloniale,* with two mounted squadrons and one half-squadron equipped with machine guns. Following the occupation of Addis Ababa a third squadron was raised from former members of the disbanded Ethiopian Imperial Guard.

On 12 September 1936 the Eritrean military forces were absorbed, together with the Somali units, into the newly-formed *Forze Armate dell'Africa Orientale Italiana* ('Armed Forces of Italian Eastern Africa' – see below).

SOMALIA

Native infantry

The initial Italian colonization was, at least on the surface, a 'private enterprise' by a commercial firm run by a sea-captain and businessman named Vincenzo Filonardi. In 1884 he obtained some concessions at Mogadishu and in the Benadir region inland from the coast, and his company hired local guards previously employed by the Sultanate of Zanzibar. By 1894 these numbered about 680 men, who lacked either training or discipline. After Filonardi's territory passed to Italian government administration in 1889, in 1903 Italian officers from Eritrea were sent to Somalia to organize a colonial force.

On 15 April 1904 this became the *Corpo delle Guardie del Benadir*, with 12 regular infantry companies. Of inconsistent strength, these were consolidated into three companies during 1905. In 1908, when separate territories in Somalia were unified into a single colony, the force was retitled the *Regio Corpo Truppe Coloniali della Somalia Italiana* ('Royal Colonial Troops Corps of Italian Somalia'). By that time there were six companies, and the number continued to increase from 1908. Of 16 companies existing in 1914, three were disbanded in 1916 for reasons of cost. The Somali infantrymen performed well during a long struggle conducted jointly by the Italians and the authorities in British Somaliland against the religious leader Sheikh Mohammed ben Aballah ('the Mad Mullah') until his death in 1921.

Somalia, like Eritrea, had to contribute to the counter-insurgency in Libya. From March 1913, three or four infantry companies at a time were grouped into successive *I, II* and *III Battaglioni Benadir* which were sent to fight the Libyan resistance. The first two were short-lived, but the four-company *III Battaglione Benadir* opeated from 1914 to 1921. Their good service persuaded the authorities to form permanent three-company battalions in Somalia from 1925.The first three Somali Native Battalions were followed by three more in 1926, but in 1928, for economic reasons, V and VI Bns were disbanded. In 1931 so too were III and IV Bns, but only for a few months, while V and VI Bns were re-raised only in 1935 at the outbreak of war with Ethiopia. From 1928 the number of companies in three of the remaining units was increased to four, of which one was formed from *amhara* soldiers (the term for Eritreans or Ethiopians living in Somalia). From 1929 one of the four in each battalion became an MG company, but in 1930 the number of rifle companies in each unit was reduced from three to two. During the 1935 mobilization for Ethiopia, another six battalions of Somali infantry were raised, bringing the total to 12; again of mixed composition, these are sometimes termed 'Arab-Somali' battalions.

In addition, some independent companies performed garrison duties: the Independent Company of Migiurtinia (from 1931); the Independent Co of Nogal (1928-30); the Presidial Co of Mogadishu (of veterans, from 1926); and the Presidial Co of Mogadishu (from 1913 – a depot company for training recruits). In 1912 the first two independent machine-gun sections were organized, followed by another 14 during the years 1913–18. In 1925–26 these were all absorbed into the re-organized infantry battalions, but during 1935 another five independent sections were raised for the war in Ethiopia.

Sciumbasci (left) and *muntaz* from one of the *amhara* (Eritrean/Ethiopian) companies used to fill out Somali native infantry battalions. Both wear the 1928 lengthened modification of the standing-collar M1913 khaki jacket, over the white blouse and trousers. The senior NCO has knee-high black leather gaiters, and note the large T-pommel of his curved knife. The crosses hanging from the necks of both soldiers suggest that they are Christian Ethiopians.

Supporting arms

In 1896, a first 20-man experimental scouting platoon of camel troops was raised. In 1911 a *Squadrone Cammellieri* was formed; sent to Libya in 1913, that December it was transferred to the establishment of the Cyrenaican governorate.

A single four-section colonial artillery company was organized in 1906, and in 1909 one section was given mules to transport light guns. Two camel sections were formed in 1925 and 1926, and the mule section also converted to camels, bringing the Somali artillery to a total of seven positional sections and three *Sezioni Cammellate*. In 1927 these categories were expanded, respectively, to 18 and 7 sections, each with two artillery pieces and two machine guns. Soon, however, the camel sections were separated from the rest to form an independent group with four batteries (increased to seven in 1935); the 18 positional sections were reduced to 14, and later to 8. In 1929 the Somali artillery was reorganized into three camel batteries and five positional sections. A single motorized company was added in 1931, which was expanded to become a three-battery group in 1935. A single *Compagnia Specialisti del Genio* – a company of Somali engineers led by Italian officers and NCOs – was formed only in 1931.

In 1926 a first squadron of armoured cars was organized, followed by a second in 1932; each had five Autoblindo Lancia 1Z cars. In 1934 a single *Compagnia Carri Veloci* with two platoons of CV33 tankettes was organized, and this soon absorbed the armoured cars to form a single unit. With the outbreak of the Ethiopian campaign in 1935, this was expanded into the *Raggruppamento Carri d'Assalto della Somalia* ('Somalian Assault Tank Group'), with three companies of tankettes and one section of armoured cars.

Paramilitaries and auxiliaries

These were similar but not identical to those in Eritrea, starting in 1907 with the *Regio Corpo di Polizia Indigena*, mainly recruited from former guards employed by the Compagnia Filonardi. After several changes of title these urban gendarmes became the *Corpo Zaptiè della Somalia Italiana* in 1923. By 1927 it comprised an impressive 1,500 men, but (due, once again, to Italy's chronic economic problems) it was reduced to 400 during 1928-31. In 1935 the Somali police were reorganized as a 'division' of the *Carabinieri Reali (Divisione CC. RR. della Somalia)*.

During 1924, the authorities organized a single horsed platoon of 25 picked veterans to act as the governor's mounted bodyguard – the *Plotone Zaptiè Guardie del Governatore*. In 1936, following the creation of Italian East Africa, these Somali guardsmen became the new *Scorta Vicereale* ('Viceroy's Escort') stationed in Addis Ababa. From 1938 the unit began to accept some Eritrean gendarmes, and in 1939 it consisted of one Eritrean squadron and one Somali company, with (as in all colonial units) Italian officers. A 25-man *Corpo di Guardie Doganali* supported the small team from the Italian *Guardia di Finanza* stationed in Somalia; they were later increased to 200, before finally being disbanded in 1936.

Away from the urban centres, the vast hinterland of Somalia was patrolled by an independent corps of rural police known as the *Gogle*. These semi-regular bands, recruited from friendly tribes, carried out functions including guarding the precious waterholes, or escorting

Bulukbasci of the Somali 1st Native Bn in 1939, wearing M1928 khaki dress with falling collar and four box-pleated pockets. For colours, compare with Plate D2; the waist-sash here appears to be red, as worn by all these units until the introduction of individual unit colours from 1925. The embroidered crown badge on his brassards indicates a promotion for courage in battle.

travelling Italians. The *Gogle* was divided into *Bande di Cabila* (tasked with patrolling the countryside), or *Bande di Confine* (tasked with protecting the extensive frontier with Ethiopia). The former were disbanded during 1920-23, while the latter were reorganized as the new *Dubat* corps in 1924.

Since Somalia's very long border with Ethiopia was frequently crossed by large bands of cattle-rustlers, it was decided in 1924 to create a more effective and militarized frontier force termed the *Bande Armate di Confine,* or *Bande Dubat.* These consisted of groups of 40-50 men recruited from warlike tribes, accustomed to travelling long distances on foot, and equipped as highly mobile light infantrymen. Despite their only 'semi-regular' status the *Dubat* soon proved to be excellent fighters, and during 1925-26 the number of bands was rapidly expanded to reach a total of 50. At their peak the *Dubat* were about 3,000 strong, including some *Dubor* camel-mounted bands. In 1931 the establishment was reduced to 1,000 fighters, and the *Dubat* began to be misemployed on duties such as road-building. However, the 1935 mobilization saw them greatly enlarged into an independent command of six *Gruppi Bande Dubat*, which were employed with great success as light infantry.

Ascaro (left) and *bulukbasci* of the Somali 1st Camel Artillery Battery, 1931. Both wear the updated version of the M1913 khaki uniform, with yellow cap-tassels and waist-sashes. In 1935 the four batteries of the Camel Artillery Group were increased to seven.

Like Eritrea, Somalia had a *Milizia Mobile,* which was organized in 1912. However, this had only a single infantry company, and was never mobilized for field service. In 1933 the Italians created a new corps of *Fucilieri Indigeni Volontari* ('Native Volunteer Riflemen') as a general reserve for use in emergencies, but these were only liable for one month's service. During 1934 a total of 2,000 volunteers were enlisted.

Again as in Eritrea, the Italians had formed a network of alliances with local rulers. They were never able to organize an effective system of *Bande Irregolari* in Somalia, but before 1908 some 'centuries' of irregular warriors could be found among the regular colonial units.

Oltregiuba

OPPOSITE
A Somali *Dubat* crew training with a Fiat-Revelli M1914 machine gun. This became common in the African colonies after the metropolitan *Regio Esercito* re-equipped in 1919 and passed its previous weapons over to the colonial troops.

In 1925, Britain ceded to Italy a region of eastern Kenya known as Jubaland or the *Oltregiuba.* For nearly two years before its annexation to Somalia in 1926, this territory had its own independent *Regio Corpo di Occupazione dell'Oltregiuba* ('Royal Occupation Corps of the Oltregiuba'), This comprised: six infantry companies (five of Somalis, and one of *amhara* soldiers); nine machine-gun sections; an artillery company (with four positional sections and one camel section), and a 140-strong police company of *zaptiè.*

UN Trust Territory of Somaliland, 1949–60

Very few people, even in Italy, know that Somalia remained under Italian control until 1960. In 1947 the Treaty of Paris freed Libya from Italian colonial control, and allocated Eritrea to Ethiopia. Somalia, however, was transformed by the United Nations into the Trust Territory of Somaliland. From 21 November 1949, the UN assigned this to Italian control while it carried out the constitutional processes which would culminate in its union with British Somaliland in 1960, to form the independent Republic of Somalia.

The Italian government soon organized a small *Corpo di Sicurezza* ('Security Corps') that was sent to the Horn of Africa during 1950. This comprised: four squadrons of armoured cavalry, each with two Staghound armoured-car platoons and one Sherman tank platoon; three battalions of *Carabinieri*, each with three rifle companies and one armoured company; one battery of field artillery; and two companies of engineers.

In addition to the above, the Italians seconded a number of officers who were tasked with organizing and training new Somali military forces. They first recruited a large number of former *ascari* veterans of the 1940–41 campaigns, and employed them as NCO cadres for the new units that were in the process of being formed. This strong armature allowed the rapid creation of four infantry battalions, of which the 4th was transformed into a training unit during 1952; the other three each had three rifle companies. Over time other units were organized, and received the equipment brought from Italy by the original Security Corps. These included a four-platoon squadron of armoured cars, a field artillery section, a company of engineers and a company of military police; an additional three camel companies were also organized. By the end of 1955 most of the Italian troops had already left Somalia, and in 1960 the forces of the new republic initially retained the military structure which they had introduced during 1950–55.

ABOVE
Somali *zaptiè* in 1914, when these gendarmes were still collectively known as the *Regio Corpo di Polizia Indigena*. He is dressed similarly to the contemporary Somali infantry, but his service is identified by the white-metal *Carabinieri* flaming-grenade badge on his *tarbusc*. His red waistcoat has white edging and 'knot' embroidery, and his long white blouse has red collar patches. A red waist-sash, white trousers and brown sandals complete his uniform.

ITALIAN EAST AFRICA, 1936–41

Unification of forces

On 12 September 1936, following the proclamation of the Italian Empire and the unification of all the Italian colonies in North-East Africa into a single administrative entity *(Africa Orientale Italiana)*, the colonial forces of Eritrea and Somalia were ordered amalgamated into a new structure termed the *Forze Armate dell'Africa Orientale Italiana*. Italian East Africa also included the vast newly-conquered territories of Ethiopia, and Mussolini hoped to recruit many new colonial units from among their populations – being apparently oblivious of the hatred in which the invaders were held by very many Ethiopians. In several peripheral areas substantial bands of insurgents were still active against the Italians, and Ethiopia was never fully pacified. Even so a significant number of units were raised there before June 1940.

The Military Forces of Italian East Africa were organized during 1937, after the unified Italian colony was restructured into five autonomous administrative entities (see map, page 5): Eritrea; Amhara (northern Ethiopia); Galla-Sidama (south-western Ethiopia); Harar (south-eastern Ethiopia); and Somalia. The colonial infantry was reorganized and expanded into a total of 16 *brigate indigene,* each comprising four infantry battalions, one field battery, two mortar batteries, and one engineer company. Each infantry battalion had three rifle companies and one machine-gun company. In some brigades one of the infantry battalions was replaced by a two-squadron cavalry group. In all, the 16 native brigades totalled 58 infantry battalions and 5 cavalry groups; 10 of the brigades had four infantry battalions; 5 brigades had three battalions and one cavalry group; and a single brigade just three infantry battalions. They were distributed among the five administrative regions: 3 brigades in Eritrea, 4 in Amhara, 4 in Galla-Sidama, 3 in Harar, and 2 in Somalia.

During the years 1938–40 the Italians expanded their forces by recruiting new native units from the conquered regions of Ethiopia. In this way the total of *brigate indigene* was increased to 25, and that of cavalry groups to 16. During the 1940 mobilization for World War II another 10 colonial brigades, totalling 42 infantry battalions, were organized to fight against the British. Native troops far outnumbered the few metropolitan formations deployed to East Africa: two infantry divisions, and 25 battalions of Fascist Party MVSN militia (the latter grouped into the 'Blackshirts African Group of Battalions'). The Army's 40th Inf Div bore the colonial denomination 'Cacciatori d'Africa', but in fact, like the 65th Inf Div 'Granatieri di Savola', it consisted entirely of Italian metropolitan units. The order of battle in East Africa during June 1940 was as follows:

(continued on page 33)

Ethiopian irregular of the *Bande Irregolari* raised during the war of 1935–36. Dressed in the traditional cotton *shamma* garment over a jacket and trousers, he is armed with a long *shotel* sabre as well as an old Vetterli-Vitali M1870/87 rifle provided by the Italian authorities.

24

ERITREA, 1887–1911
1: *Basci buzuk, Orda Esterna*, 1887
2: Chasseur, 1st Regt, *Cacciatori d'Africa,* 1888
3: *Ascaro,* Native Cav Sqn 'Asmara', 1893–94

A

ERITREA, 1912–1935
1: Ascaro, 1st Mtn Arty Bty, 1912
2: Zaptié, Compagnia CC. RR., 1912
3: Muntaz, 14th Native Bn, 1935

B

SOMALIA, 1906–25
1: Ascaro, Native Arty Co, 1906
2: Zaptié, Governor's Mtd Bodyguard, 1924
3: Capo comandante, 1st Group *Dubat*, 1925

C

SOMALIA, 1926–60
1: *Ascaro,* Armoured Car Sqn, 1931
2: *Muntaz,* MG Co, 11th Native Bn, 1941
3: *Muntaz,* 1st Somali Bn; UN Trust Somaliland, 1953

D

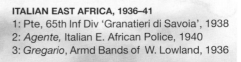

ITALIAN EAST AFRICA, 1936–41
1: Pte, 65th Inf Div 'Granatieri di Savoia', 1938
2: *Agente,* Italian E. African Police, 1940
3: *Gregario*, Armd Bands of W. Lowland, 1936

LIBYA, 1912–33
1: *Muntaz*, 6th Native Bn;
Cyrenaica, 1916
2: *Savaro*, 1st Sqn; Tripolitania,
1926
3: *Spahis*, 1st Group;
Tripolitania, 1929

LIBYA, 1934–42

1: *Muntaz, 7th Native Bn, 1940*

2: *Bulukbasci, Meharisti, 1st Saharan Grp, 1935*

3: *Ascaro, Para Training Bn 'Air Infantry', 1938–39*

H

Northern Theatre

Eritrea
5th, 8th & 12th Native Brigades
Armoured car section 'Eritrea'
Amhara
3rd, 4th, 19th, 21st & 22nd
   Native Bdes
Armd car section 'Amhara'

Southern Theatre

Galla-Sidama
1st, 9th, 10th, 18th & 25th
   Native Bdes
Armd car section 'Galla-Sidama'
Giuba
91st & 92nd Native Bdes
Armd car section 'Giuba'

Eastern Theatre

Scioa
20th & 23rd Native Bdes
Blackshirts African Grp of Bns
Armd car section 'Scioa'
Harar
13th-15th & 17th Native Bdes
1st Armd Car Sqn
Armd car section 'Harar'

General Reserve

40th Inf Div 'Cacciatori d'Africa'
65th Inf Div 'Granatieri di Savoia'
2nd , 6th, 7th, 11th, 16th,
   41st & 85th Native Bdes
1st & 2nd Special Light Tank Cos

As is clear from the above, the numbering of the *brigate indigene* was not entirely sequential, since the organization of seven of the new brigades was not completed before Italy's entry into the war. As for armour, the two Light Tank Cos were equipped with the CV33 tankette, although it is recorded that there were also 24 M11/39 medium tanks in East Africa. The 1st Armd Car Sqn had the Fiat 611, while the various regional sections had the Lancia 1ZM.

Paramilitaries and auxiliaries

In 1936, following the conquest of Ethiopia, the Italian government decided to organize a large corps of *Polizia dell'Africa Italiana* to serve as the militarized police force throughout its North and East African possessions. This was structured in seven battalions, plus a special mounted squadron to provide a ceremonial bodyguard for the Italian viceroy in Addis Ababa. The 'Police of Italian Africa' would contribute the independent *Battaglione 'Romolo Gessi'* to the war against Britain in North Africa. Trained for deep reconnaissance and counter-insurgency, this had two motorcycle companies and one with armoured cars, and it distinguished itself until finally disbanded in January 1942.

An Ethiopian 'Irregular Band' being transported to the front in an Italian lorry during the war of 1935–36. They are all wearing their civilian clothing, and most seem to be armed with spears rather than rifles.

An Italian officer with two Ethiopian irregulars, photographed in Amhara during 1939. The officer wears the M1934 *Sahariana* jacket; distinguishable by the chest yoke incorporating the flaps of the breast pockets, this was not used by NCOs and privates. One of the Ethiopians carries a Breda 6.5mm M1930 light machine gun.

The creation of the *Polizia dell'Africa Italiana* did not cause the disbandment of the *zaptiè* urban gendarmerie; this had been greatly expanded during 1935-40, and by the outbreak of war it had 3,500 policemen organized in six *Gruppi* corresponding to the six regions of Italian East Africa. The *zaptiè* provided one combat company, which was assembled with two companies of Italian *Carabinieri* to form an

Ascari of the 44th Native Bn, one of the new infantry units created after the conquest of Ethiopia. All are wearing M1928 khaki uniforms, and have belt equipment for the M1891 Carcano rifle. For some reason the central figure is wearing a khaki fatigue cap on top of his *tarbusc.* One source suggests that the 44th Bn may have worn a waist-sash horizontally striped yellow and purple.

independent battalion. This was one of the last Italian units to surrender to the British in 1941, after three months of stubborn resistance.

From 1936, most of the irregular tribal allies which had been attracted to the Italian cause during the invasion of Ethiopia were diverted towards the recruiting effort for the new native military units. However, some Ethiopian *Bande Irregolari* were retained, and some of the effective Eritrean *Bande Armate* and Somali *Bande Dubat* were also deployed for guerrilla work during 1940–41.

LIBYA

Infantry

The Italians had limited success in raising Libyan native units until after the final defeat of tribal resistance in about 1930. Prior to that, only the surroundings of the major coastal cities, which remained under Italian control during World War I, provided a certain number of recruits, and even there Cyrenaica – which retained a stronger Ottoman influence – was always less productive. (It should be borne in mind that for decades the governorates, and thus the forces, of Tripolitania and Cyrenaica remained separate entities, reflecting the age-old cultural differences between western and eastern Libya which persist to this day.)

On 20 August 1912 a first native infantry battalion was organized in the Tripoli area, numbering 1,000 soldiers in four companies. During the following months another four similar battalions were raised in Tripolitania. The first three Cyrenaican battalions were created in 1913. Originally 14 Libyan infantry battalions had been planned, but only 10 had been raised by the outbreak of World War I (6 in Tripolitania and 4 in Cyrenaica), plus one independent company stationed in the southern region of Fezzan.

During 1915–16 the Libyan battalions suffered such heavy losses at the hands of the Senussi rebels that they had to be transferred to Sicily for reorganization. When the Great War ended, two of the Tripolitanian units had to be disbanded, while three of those from Cyrenaica each had to

Libyan infantrymen of the 7th Native Bn on parade in 1929, still wearing the old white uniform with coloured waistcoats that was introduced during 1912. Compare with Plate F1 for general appearance, but here the waistcoat is light blue with red embroidery, and the waist-sash (obscured here) is vertically striped light blue/ red.

be filled out with two companies of Eritrean *ascari*, and each battalion was reduced to three rifle companies plus a machine-gun section. This manpower shortfall led to the disbandment of three of the four Cyrenaican battalions during 1921–23. During 1924 one more unit was organized in Tripolitania, while during 1926 one platoon of invalids was raised in each of the governorates. In 1927 a general improvement in the military situation made it possible to raise yet another battalion in Tripolitania and two in Cyrenaica, and the machine-gun section of each unit was expanded to company size. During 1929–30, following the pacification of most of Libya, two battalions were disbanded in Tripolitania and three in Cyrenaica (one of which was reduced to an independent company).

Following unification during 1934, on 12 September 1935 the colonial forces of Tripolitania and Cyrenaica were amalgamated into a single structure, which was to comprise three regiments and two independent companies from Tripolitania, and three regiments from Cyrenaica, each of two battalions. However, in two of the Tripolitanian regiments one of the battalions was made up of Eritrean *ascari*, while two of the three Cyrenaican regiments were entirely Eritrean. This Eritrean contribution of 6 out of the 12 battalions underlines the relative weakness of Libyan recruitment.

For the invasion of Ethiopia in 1935 Libya was required to provide an infantry division, and mobilized its 1st, 3rd and 4th Native Infantry Regiments. After their return in 1937, the Libyan colonial infantry was completely reorganized. The six existing regiments were disbanded, and a new structure produced eight battalions (each with three rifle and one machine-gun companies), plus one independent heavy machine-gun company. During 1938-39 the number of heavy MG companies was increased to eight, and one was attached to each infantry battalion.

With the outbreak of World War II in 1939, Mussolini ordered the rapid expansion of the Libyan infantry. Consequently, by the time Italy abandoned its neutrality in June 1940, 12 infantry battalions and 9 heavy MG companies were grouped into two Libyan divisions.

1st Libyan Division	**2nd Libyan Division**
I Libyan Infantry Group	*III Libyan Inf Grp*
III, IV & XIX Native Bns	VI, VII & XIV Native Bns
II Libyan Inf Grp	*IV Libyan Inf Grp*
VIII, XVII & XVIII Native Bns	II, XV & XVI Native Bns
I Libyan Artillery Group	*II Libyan Arty Group*
I & II Field Batteries	III & IV Field Btys
I Anti-Aircraft Bty	II AA Bty
(plus)	*(plus)*
I Anti-Tank Bty	II AT Bty
I Engineer Company	II Eng Co

During autumn 1940 to spring 1941 the Italians raised another four active and four depot battalions, which joined the campaigns against the British in North Africa. By January 1942 the Libyan units had been practically destroyed, and the surviving elements had to be completely reorganized in just five battalions, each with four rifle companies. After the battle of El Alamein in October–November 1942 what remained of the independent MG companies were grouped to form two battalions, which were wiped out, together with the other Libyan infantry units, during the early months of 1943.

Supporting arms: cavalry

The Libyan colonial cavalry comprised two distinct categories: the *Savari*, which received European training and Italian equipment, and the *Spahi*, which followed their indigenous light-cavalry traditions and rode their own horses.

Shortly after their first landings in 1911 the Italians recruited some 600 tribal horsemen from around Tripoli, initially organized as three 'semi-regular' *bande*. Some time later, a single squadron was raised from the vicinity of Benghazi (these were the first to be known as *savari*). During 1912 the Tripolitanian cavalrymen were also reorganized as one squadron of S*avari*, but after a few months the Italians decided to replace both these units with a new organization. This created six squadrons of *Savari* (three each in Tripolitania and Cyrenaica).

Following World War I the number of *Savari* squadrons was progressively increased to seven in Tripolitania and five in Cyrenaica. By 1928 Tripolitania had been completely pacified, so during 1929-30 the seven squadrons there were reduced to two. In 1935 all the Libyan *Savari* were assembled into a single four-squadron *Gruppo Squadroni*.

The Libyan *Spahi* were created during World War I, to provide a cheap and highly mobile force to answer the hit-and-run tactics of the Senussi rebels. They were also initially employed to patrol the long western border between Tripolitania and French-ruled Tunisia, across which the Libyan insurgents received most of their weapons and supplies. The irregular *Spahi* were armed with rifles but not sabres, and were mainly employed as mounted skirmishers. A first group of 150 riders was organized on 22 September 1916, followed by a second group in 1917 and a third during 1919, and each was allocated its own patrol sector along the Tunisian frontier. During 1927–29 the Italians failed in an effort to form three more groups on Cyrenaica's eastern border with Egypt. In 1932 one of the three Tripolitanian groups was disbanded; but in 1938 the remaining two (termed 'squadrons' since 1934) were expanded to four, and were assembled to form a single *Gruppo Squadroni*. During 1940–41 the *Spahi* were again greatly increased, to form three Groups of Squadrons having three squadrons each.

Ascari **of, again, the Libyan 7th Native Bn, but photographed in 1934. They wear the new M1928 khaki uniform (compare with Plate G1), and the waist-sash is clearly visible. The** *gagliardetto* **(small flag, guidon) is also striped light blue/ red, and bears centrally a large number 'VII' embroidered in black.**

A *spahis* light cavalryman of the short-lived groups raised in Cyrenaica during 1927-29. Except for the red *tachia* he wears civilian clothing, including a white *parasia* wrapped around his torso. His weapon is the usual issue M1891 Carcano carbine, but his horse furniture is Arab – compare with Plate F3.

Camel troops

The Libyan cavalry's first squadron of *meharisti* camel troops was organized in November 1913, followed by a second early in 1914. In 1916, these were reorganized as a single squadron with three platoons. This was employed mainly for reconnaissance, or to escort Italian columns venturing into the desert. In 1924, when the Italian focus was on defeating the Senussi in the vast emptiness of Fezzan, the single squadron was disbanded and three new *Gruppi Sahariani* were organized. Each of these was a sort of self-sufficient task force designed for long desert operations, and comprised: three camel-mounted platoons (one trained to fight as cavalry, the other two as mounted infantry); one platoon on foot; one heavy machine-gun section, and one light MG section transported on camels. With the passage of time, the light MG section was replaced by a camel-borne mountain artillery section. All these units were raised in Tripolitania, as were four more created during 1927-30. In Cyrenaica, the first two permanent squadrons of *meharisti* were formed only in 1925. These were expanded into three *Gruppi Sahariani* during 1930–31, but by 1933 only one of these was still operational.

In 1935 the *meharisti* of Tripolitania and Cyrenaica were assembled together and reorganized into six groups. During 1936 these *Gruppi Sahariani* were replaced in their turn with three new independent and nominally motorized *Compagnie Auto-Sahariane* (in fact each *compagnia* was a mixed unit, with two of its three platoons retaining camels and only one entirely motorized). The companies also had attached Caproni

Ca 309 'Ghibli' aircraft for long-range reconnaissance. In 1937 these Saharan Auto Cos were increased in number to five, which were grouped to form a single battalion plus one independent company. Early in World War II the Italian Army increased the flexibility of its excellent desert motorized units by recruiting two irregular bands of tribal *meharisti*.

Artillery and engineers

A first battery of Libyan artillery was organized on 16 November 1912, followed by another two during 1913. Two of these were stationed in Tripolitania and one in Cyrenaica, each region also having one train company. During 1923–24 a third battery was raised in Tripolitania, together with four companies of garrison artillery stationed on the coast. In 1928 a first battery transported by motor vehicles was organized; during 1929, one battery was disbanded and another received camels. In 1932 the artillery of Tripolitania was completely reorganized as follows: three field batteries with camels, one garrison artillery company, and one company of the train. Soon afterwards, however, the field batteries was reduced to two, and two new garrison batteries were organized. Cyrenaica raised a second field battery only in 1927, together with three companies of garrison artillery.

With the unification of the governorates in 1934–35 the Libyan artillery was re-structured in two regiments. The first, stationed in Tripoli, comprised: one group with three camel batteries, one group with three field batteries, and a third with two howitzer batteries. The second regiment, in Benghazi, had one group with two motor batteries and a second with three camel batteries. In December 1937 both regiments were dispersed in independent groups. By March 1941 the Libyan artillery had been completely destroyed by the British advance.

A regiment of Libyan engineers (actually, mostly Italians) was raised in 1935, and its two battalions soon became autonomous units, one in Tripoli and the other in Benghazi. Each had one company of sappers, one of telegraphists and one of radio operators.

Minor units

During the Senussi insurgency in 1919, five new units of Italian *Cacciatori d'Africa* were created – two battalions in Tripolitania, supported by an armoured car squadron, and three in Cyrenaica with two armoured car companies. Over the following decade the battalions were progressively disbanded as pacification was achieved, but the three armoured-car elements survived into World War II.

The governor-general of Libya from 1934 was Air Marshal Italo Balbo, one of the world's leading air-power theorists. Simultaneously C-in-C of the *Regia Aeronautica*, in 1938 he used his authority to found a parachuting school at Castel Benito airfield, Tripoli. There he created, on 28 March, a 330-strong Italian-led volunteer Parachute Training Bn 'Air Infantry' *(Fanti dell'Aria)*, commanded by LtCol

Sciumbasci of the Libyan *meharisti,* photographed during the final campaigns in Fezzan in 1928. The traditional uniform was a turban, *suria* (blouse) and *sirual* (loose trousers), all in shades of khaki. Note the long coloured scarf crossed on his chest, and the *curbasc,* a long whip of hardened leather, hanging from his wrist. The Libyan dromedary is an animal of impressive size, capable of great physical endurance. (Compare with Plate G2.)

Meharisti of the independent Fezzan Company, photographed in 1938 wearing all-white parade dress. Some carry the M1891 Carcano infantry rifle, others the shortened version 'for special troops'. The flag is black with white Arabic inscriptions.

Tonini. A second battalion was ordered raised in April 1939, for a planned 1st Libyan Parachute Regt 'Air Infantry' of two three-company battalions, but by the end of the year this plan had been replaced with an attempt to raise the battalion from Italian volunteers instead. The unit's anticipated mission of drops behind enemy lines was abandoned after Marshal Balbo's death on 28 June 1940 (at the hands of Italian AA gunners in Tobruk), and the available personnel formed a *Gruppo Mobile 'Tonini'* as conventional light infantry. Deployed to Derna on the Cyrenaican coast, it was almost destroyed there in January 1941 during Gen O'Connor's advance, and the survivors surrendered when Beda Fomm also fell on 6 February.

Paramilitaries and auxiliaries

Initially Libya had a corps of former Ottoman gendarmes, known as *polices*. In 1912 the *Carabinieri* organized four companies of *zaptiè* in Tripolitania and some small detachments in Cyrenaica. Known for their loyalty, by 1914 these numbered 100 men on foot and 800 mounted. A fifth company and a camel-mounted group were added in Tripolitania in 1929; during the years that followed the number of companies was increased to seven, plus a special mounted platoon for the governor of Tripoli's bodyguard. In Cyrenaica the initial detachments were gradually expanded into four companies. By 1940, seven *zaptiè* companies were deployed throughout Libya, and a single 150-man squadron was mobilized to fight the British. (Of the seven battalions that made up the *Polizia dell'Africa Italiana* organized in 1936, only one was stationed in Libya.)

During World War I, the Italians had recruited a large number of tribal irregulars to fight against the Senussi, and their successes led to the creation of three larger *Gruppi Ausiliari;* meanwhile, smaller *Bande*

Indigene were limited to secondary duties such as guarding cattle and escorting convoys. In 1930 the Italian authorities began to gather several thousand irregulars into four Groups, and by 1932 the individual *Bande* had practically disappeared. Some horse- and camel-mounted bands began to be re-raised in 1940, to counter pro-French and pro-British *bedouin*.

SELECT BIBLIOGRAPHY

Ales, S., Crociani, P. & Viotti, A., *Struttura, uniformi, distintivi ed insegne delle Truppe Libiche 1912-1943* (Ufficio Storico dello Stato Maggiore dell'Esercito, 2012)

Ales, S. & Viotti, A., *Struttura, uniformi e distintivi dell'Esercito Italiano 1946-1970* (Ufficio Storico dello Stato Maggiore dell'Esercito, 2007)

Compagni, P. & Scollo, L., *I Bersaglieri 1836-2007: storia e uniformi del corpo dalla fondazione ad oggi* (Itinera Progetti, 2009)

Crociani, P. & Battistelli, P.P., *Italian Army Elite Units & Special Forces 1940-43,* Elite 99 (Osprey Publishing, 2011)

Gibellini, Valerio, *Il Soldato Italiano dal 1909 al 1945* (Rivista Militare, 1988)

McLachlan, Sean, *Armies of the Adowa Campaign 1896,* MAA 471 (Osprey Publishing, 2011)

Nicolle, David, *The Italian Invasion of Abyssinia 1935-36,* MAA 309 (Osprey Publishing, 1997)

Nicolle, David, *Lawrence and the Arab Revolts,* MAA 208 (Osprey Publishing, 1989)

Palieri, Mario, *Note per la Storia del Regio Corpe Truppe Coloniali della Somalia Italiana* (Tipografia Editrice Schioppo, 1929)

Rosignoli, Guido, *Alpini: uniformi, distintivi, equipaggiamento ed armi dalla costituzione ai giorni nostri* (Ermanno Albertelli Editore, 2002)

Viotti, Andrea, *L'Uniforme Grigio-Verde 1909–1918* (Ufficio Storico dello Stato Maggiore dell'Esercito, 2013)

Zorzetto, Gabriele, *Bande Regolari e Irregolari nella campagna A.O. 1935–1936* (Edizioni Museo dell'Araba Fenice, 2019)

Zorzetto, Gabriele, *Penne di Falco. La cavalleria dell'Africa Orientale 1888–1941* (Edizioni Museo dell'Araba Fenice, 2019)

Zorzetto, Gabriele, *Cavalleria Libica 1911–1943, Uniformi e Insegne* (Edizioni Museo dell'Araba Fenice, 2020)

Zorzetto, Gabriele, *Uniformi e Insegne delle Truppe Coloniali Italiane: Eritrea e Somalia, 1885–1934* (Edizioni Museo dell'Araba Fenice, 2011)

An Italian officer of the *Carabinieri Reali* photographed with Libyan mounted *zaptiè* in about 1920. The mounted gendarmes wear khaki uniforms like those of *Savari* regular cavalry, but with the flaming-grenade badge on the *taohia*, an all-red waist sash, and red jacket collars with two silver-braid stripes. The officer has the *Carabinieri* badge, set on the national cockade, on his sun-helmet; his khaki jacket is the M1887 with frontal pleats, and he too has a silver-braided red collar, but also pointed red cuffs.

OPPOSITE
Libyan artillerymen serving a 65/17 'infantry gun', which had originally been designed as a mountain artillery piece transportable on mules. These soldiers wear M1928 khaki uniform, as in Plate G1.

PLATE COMMENTARIES

A: ERITREA, 1887–1911

A1: *Basci buzuk, Orda Esterna,* 1887

Initially the *basci buzuk* wore semi-civilian dress of a red *tarbusc* with a black or dark blue tassel, a white knee-length blouse, loose white trousers (often rolled up), and brown sandals, with a coloured waist-sash. From 1887 the members of the *Orda Interna* wore a blue scarf around their *tarbusc*, while the *Orda Esterna* were identified by green. Rank, if any, was shown by a simple black patch on the right sleeve, bearing different numbers of red stars. The coloured waist-sashes came to be adopted as a fundamental element of Italian colonial uniforms, the colours and patterns being varied to identify the different units (see under Plate B3) . On formal occasions the *basci buzuk* might wear over his blouse a dark blue jacket decorated with red trim and yellow piping. This man's main weapon is the single-shot Remington 'rolling block' rifle, produced in .43in calibre for the Egyptian Army; most irregulars also carried curved sabres and/or knives.

A2: Private, 1st Regiment, *Cacciatori d'Africa*, 1888

The early uniform of the Italian 'African Chasseurs' included an M1887 cork helmet, bearing a crowned white-metal frontal badge of two bugle-horns set on the Italian red/white/green national cockade. The Chasseurs' single black feather, rising from a red pompon, was clearly inspired by the raven feather worn on their headgear by the metropolitan *Alpini* (mountain infantry). On the fold-down collar of the white tropical jacket are the five-point white-metal Savoy stars of the *Regio Esercito* (Italian 'Royal Army'). Note the front skirt corners buttoned up to clear the cartridge pouch worn on a waist belt, and also the slung 1876 canteen and off-white haversack. The rifle is a bolt-action 10.4mm Vetterli-Vitali M1870/87 with a four-round magazine.

In 1889 the *Cacciatori d'Africa* received a new M1887 khaki ('light bronze') linen uniform, including a helmet cover. The M1887 jacket had shoulder straps; a standing collar (though often opened and worn folded down) with white cloth stars; two 'Norfolk-style' pleats down the front; and, for NCOs and warrant officers, red points-up chevrons on both forearms, with a tall loop extending from the top chevron. This uniform also appeared in white for barracks dress. In 1894 a new model of cork helmet was introduced, worn by that date with a green feather *panache*. In the same year officers received a parade uniform of a dark blue 'patrol jacket' with black frontal frogging, and dark blue trousers.

A3: *Ascaro, Squadrone di Cavalleria Indigena 'Asmara',* 1893–94

This is the first uniform adopted by the Eritrean cavalry. The scarves wrapped around the red *tarbusc* cap were in identifying colours for the Asmara and Keren squadrons. Through this is pinned a crowned white-metal lancers' badge, and a single hawk feather was attached at the back (hence the Eritrean cavalrymens' nickname of '*Penne di Falco*'). From about 1890 the Eritrean *ascari,* both foot and mounted, began to wear this simple white waist-length 'stable jacket' instead of the previous knee-length blouse (see A1); from 1904 ranks were indicated by red points-up sleeve chevrons, and later the same number of silver stars appeared on the

front of their headgear. They also began using canvas leggings (though foot soldiers continued to march barefoot, and troopers rode without boots or spurs). Initially the horsemen were armed only with sabre and carbine (here, the 6.5mm M1891 *moschetto da cavalleria* with its characteristic fold-back fixed bayonet, which arrrived in 1893), but later they received cavalry lances.

In 1908 the cavalry adopted a khaki jacket which differed from that of the infantry (see under Plate B3) in that it retained the frontal pleats of the Italian 1887 design; this was also produced in a white parade version. The subsequent M1928 cavalry jacket was also produced in both khaki service and white parade versions. From 1913 the *Penne di Falco* replaced their old canvas leggings with new brown leather gaiters. The cavalryman's waist-sash remained red from about 1890 up until World War II.

B: ERITREA, 1912–1935

B1: *Ascaro*, 1st Mountain Artillery Battery, 1912

Eritrean artillerymen were dressed quite similarly to the infantry, their uniforms following the evolution of the latter from 1908 to 1940. From about 1890 a simple white jacket was introduced, but from 1904 that was replaced with this new model shaped like a stable jacket, with a standing collar and two pockets; it could be worn alone or, as here, over the traditional white knee-length blouse. From about 1890 the

Eritrean *sciumbasci* of the cavalry *Squadrone Indigeno* in 1913; for the *tarbusc* colours see the earlier *'Penne di Falco'* illustrated as Plate A3. This senior NCO wears the white parade version of the M1908 jacket tucked under his red waist-sash, and has just received brown leather knee-gaiters. He is armed with a holstered revolver, a carbine in a saddle-boot, and a lance with a medium blue swallow-tail pennon.

tassel of the *tarbusc* and the waist-sash worn by all *ascari* began to appear in unit identifying colours, but for the whole artillery these were black and yellow respectively. This artilleryman's main weapon is a *moschetto 91 per truppe speciali,* a shortened M1891 rifle, and his ammunition pouches are of the two-pocket bandolier type issued to mounted troops. The sabre for Eritrean and Somali artillerymen was Italian-made.

B2: *Zaptiè, Compagnia CC. RR.,* 1912

Until 1887 the *zaptiè* wore the same white uniform as the infantry, but with a red left-arm brassard embroidered in black with 'PS' (for *Pubblica Sicurezza*). In that year a new white jacket was introduced for wear over the blouse. Apart from its colour this was very similar to the M1887 khaki tunic issued to the *Cacciatori d'Africa*, with shoulder straps and two frontal pleats. With the new uniform the Eritrean gendarmes also received a red waist-sash, and a red *tarbusc* with a medium blue tassel and a white-metal frontal badge of a flaming grenade (the distinctive symbol of the Italian *Carabinieri Reali,* with whom they were now serving). From 1908 the *zaptiè* received this distinctive khaki stable jacket. The main weapon is the 6.5mm M1891 Carcano cavalry carbine (as Plate A3), but he also carries a holstered revolver, presumably the 10.35mm M1889 Glisenti.

B3: *Muntaz,* 14th Native Battalion, 1935

From 1901 a khaki campaign tunic had been introduced for Eritrean infantry, longer than the Italian M1887 and with four pockets. This was unpopular with the *ascari,* however, and from 1908 it began to be replaced with a new model which was similar, but lacked the frontal pleats of the M1887 and had different pockets. That M1908 khaki jacket was introduced on a large scale only from 1913, so the first Eritrean units sent to Libya in 1912 were still wearing the M1904 white jacket illustrated in B1. Finally, from 1928, the M1908 jacket was officially replaced with the new uniform reconstructed here, which remained in use until the fall of Italian Eastern Africa in World War II.

The red *tarbusc* is hidden here by the khaki cover that began to be issued in the early 1930s, but uncovered examples can be seen in several of the photographs; it would display a brass badge showing personal specialty (e.g. a diagonal rifle for a qualfied marksman), and silver rank stars matching the number of sleeve chevrons. In 1904 the red points-up rank chevrons previously worn on both sleeves were replaced with these black cloth triangular brassards attached temporarily with strings; here they bear the single red chevron of corporal's rank; the brass rifle specialty badge of a marksman; and two red stars indicating this re-enlisted soldier's 12 years' service.

The distinctive colours of the 14th Native Battalion, light blue/ yellow, are visible in the *tarbusc* tassel and the striped pattern of the waist-sash. Both these features dated from about 1890, and the colours of the eight senior battalions were: 1st 'Turrito', red; 2nd 'Hidalgo', azure-blue; 3rd 'Galliano', crimson; 4th 'Toselli', black; 5th 'Ameglio', a kind of multicoloured 'tartan'; 6th 'Cossu', light green, later red/ black; 7th 'Valli', white, later red/light blue; and 8th 'Gamerra', russet. After World War I most Eritrean infantrymen replaced their canvas leggings with the puttees *(fasce mollettiere)* worn by Italian metropolitan troops. Colonial troops were sometimes seen with four,

Somali *sciumbasci* of the 71st Native Bn in 1938, wearing the new version of the M1913 khaki uniform that was introduced in 1928 (see Plate D2). By the outbreak of World War II the Muslim Somali soldiers had been permitted to replace their red *tarbusc* with a khaki turban. Again, note on his triangular red-on-khaki brassard the crown badge which distinguished soldiers who had received a field promotion for personal courage; the re-enlistment stars below it seem to have white-metal badges pinned to red cloth stars. Although the waist-sash is absent here, one source gives it as amaranth-red and brown vertical stripes for the 71st Battalion.

rather than the usual two M1907 brown leather cartridge pouches. Note the slung 'horseshoe rolls' of the blanket, and a tent-section containing small kit; and a straw-covered wine bottle carried as a water canteen. The rifle is the standard 6.5mm M1891 Carcano.

C: SOMALIA, 1906–25

C1: *Ascaro,* Native Artillery Company, 1906

Until 1906 the Somali infantry and artillery did not have a proper uniform, being dressed in the red *tarbusc* with a red tassel, long white blouse, white trousers, and red waist-sash. During that year their first dress regulations were issued. These 'officialized' the previous semi-regular uniform, but added a new garment: a sleeveless waistcoat, in a distinctive colour for each infantry company, with edging and decorative embroidery in contrasting colours. For example, the 1st Native Infantry Company wore medium blue with white decorations, the 2nd Native Inf Co red trimmed with white, and so on. The cap tassel and the waist-sash remained red for all infantry companies. The artillery, as illustrated, wore a black tassel, yellow sash, and yellow waistcoat decorated with white. Rank was shown by red points-up sleeve chevrons. From 1913 the cap tassel too became yellow. This gunner's weapon is again the *moschetto 91 per truppe speciali.*

C2: *Zaptiè,* Governor's Mounted Bodyguard, 1924

This exotic special uniform in white and red was peculiar to the picked gendarmes of the small *Plotone Zaptiè Guardie del Governatore.* It would be modified in 1928, when the *tarbusc* was replaced with a red turban, and the jacket became red with yellow edging. After the foundation of Italian East Africa in 1936 the gendarmerie bodyguard was transferred to Addis Ababa, Ethiopia, to form the *Scorta Vicereale* for the Italian viceroy, who from May 1936 was the merciless Marshal Rodolfo Graziani.

The first uniform of Somali *zaptiè* was a red *tarbusc* with medium blue tassel and white-metal flaming-grenade badge; a white blouse, with red patches bearing a five-point star on the standing collar; a red waist-sash; loose white trousers and black puttees. On parade a red waistcoat with white edging and embroidery was worn over the blouse. In 1922 the gendarmes received the new khaki uniform that had been introduced for the infantry and artillery in 1913, but retained their distinctive red collar patches and waist-sash. The dress regulations of 1928 introduced a pocketless white parade version of the M1913 uniform.

As for the Somali line troops, in 1913 the infantry and artillery received a new uniform which consisted of a khaki jacket and shorts, worn with the usual red *tarbusc* and with puttees. The simple jacket had a fold-down collar, a buttoned front and two chest pockets. The cap tassel and waist-sash remained red for all infantry units until 1925, when distinctive unit combinations of colours were introduced. The dress regulations of 1928 would not modify the Somali uniforms significantly; they simply introduced a white parade version of the M1913 jacket, and the same rank-and-service sleeve brassards as used in Eritrea (see Plate B3). Khaki cap-covers were introduced during the early 1930s.

C3: *Capo comandante,* 1st Group of *Bande Dubat,* 1925

The semi-regular *Dubat* frontier guards did not have a uniform, being dressed only in a white turban and *futa* (wrap-around robe). Each 'band' included a number of *sottocapi* (corporals) and *capi* (sergeants) in addition to one *capo comandante* (commander). These warriors were distinguishable by the colours of two-tassel cords worn around the neck and torso: black for *sottocapi,* red for *capi,* and green for the *capo comandante.* The rifle is the regulation M1891 Carcano, and he carries a knife on his ammunition belt.

D: SOMALIA, 1926–60

D1: *Ascaro, Squadriglia Autoblindata,* 1931

The crews of the armoured cars deployed in Somalia wore a *casco da carrista* covered with brown leather, and this medium blue overall with two breast pockets; their identifying unit sash was vertically striped dark blue/ white. Note the mounted troops' pouch-bandolier. The few Somali tankette crewmen did not have this overall, but wore a simple white 'T-shirt' with khaki shorts, and a black waist-sash.

D2: *Muntaz,* Machine-Gun Company, 11th Native Battalion, 1941

By the outbreak of World War II the uniform of the Somali infantry had changed slightly since the M1913: under the 1928 regulations, the jacket had been lengthened and skirt pockets had been added. Also. the authorities had started permitting the Muslim soldiers of the Somali battalions to replace their red *tarbusc* with this khaki turban. Corporal's rank is shown by the single red chevron on his brassards, which also display the brass badge of a machine-gunner above the single red star indicating 2 years' service.

The short-lived colonial forces of the Oltregiuba region wore the same uniform, except for their small company of *zaptiè.* Those gendarmes wore the red *tarbusc* with medium blue tassel and white-metal grenade badge; a khaki jacket with breast pockets, and a red collar with two silver-braid stripes; red 'Austrian knots' on the sleeves (compare with Plate C2); a red waist-sash, khaki trousers and puttees, and brown leather sandals. For parade a similar white uniform was worn, but lacking the decorative sleeve knots.

D3: *Muntaz,* 1st Somali Battalion; UN Trust Territory of Somaliland, 1953

The new infantry battalions organized by the Italians in Somalia from 1950 were dressed very similarly to those existing until 1941: red *tarbusc* with tassel in battalion colours, khaki two-pocket shirt with shoulder straps, battalion waist-sash, khaki shorts and puttees, and leather sandals. The ammunition pouches were also of pre-war type. Only two of the illustrated features are new: the embroidered branch-of-service badge on the front of the cap, and a unit patch on a tab hanging from the left shoulder strap. The rifle is still the old M1891 Carcano.

The *Carabinieri* despatched to the former Italian colony were dressed quite similarly, but they wore a sun helmet of the type worn by Plate E1; distinctive collar patches, and red aiguillettes on the left shoulder; and khaki webbing gaiters with brown boots. The Somali military police working with them had medium blue cap-tassels and the white flaming-grenade badge of the *Carabinieri,* that corps' collar patches, and a red waist-sash. The members of the single armoured squadron wore a British-style drab sweater over their khaki shirt and shorts, and the US M1938 'tanker' helmet which was current Italian Army issue. The small Somali camel corps wore a khaki turban, a khaki shirt with a light blue unit badge hanging on the left sleeve, a light blue waist-sash and loose khaki trousers.

E: ITALIAN EAST AFRICA, 1936–41

E1: Infantry private, 65th Infantry Division 'Granatieri di Savoia', 1938

The two Italian infantry divisions stationed in East Africa during 1936–41 wore the standard M1934 colonial uniform that was used during the 1935-36 Italo-Ethiopian War and World War II. The cork sun helmet bore a large national cockade backing a brass arm-of-service badge, here a flaming grenade; like those of all Italian divisions, its distinctive collar patches bore the national silver star. (The single battalion of the 10th Grenadier Regt which in 1937 temporarily reinforced the Italian garrison of the Tientsin Concession in China were also dressed like this, but with standard M1931 steel helmets painted khaki and showing a black flaming grenade on the front.)

E2: *Agente, Polizia dell'Africa Orientale Italiana*, 1940
Police motorcyclists wore a brown leather crash-helmet and three-quarter length coat, the former displaying the PAI's crowned brass badge: an eagle with 'hunched' wings, and a white cross on a red cartouche on its breast. The uniform is completed with riding breeches, knee-gaiters and ankle boots. The weapon is the 9mm Beretta MAB 38A sub-machine gun, with its magazines carried in two triple canvas pouches (each set having a single strapped and buckled flap) on a broad canvas belt. The PAI's mounted ceremonial squadron paraded in a light blue turban with the brass badge and a single white feather; a white jacket with light blue collar and pointed cuffs, under a light blue waistcoat with white edging and embroidery; a light blue waist-sash; loose white trousers with a light blue side-stripe; brown leather boots; and a light blue cloak with red edging and embroidery.

E3: *Gregario,* Armed Bands of the Western Lowland, 1936
The Eritrean *Bando Armato* supported the Italian police during counter-guerrilla operations against Ethiopian insurgents. Until 1931 these semi-regular rural policemen had worn a white turban, with a white or khaki stable jacket of the 1908 model for Eritrean *zaptiè* (see Plate B2) worn over the usual white knee-length blouse. In that year, however, this new khaki uniform was introduced, with a four-pocket, stand-collar tunic, shorts and puttees. The turban and waist-sash were in identifying colours for each of the three Groups of Armed Bands: this white/ black for the Western Lowland group, white/ brown for the Eastern Lowland, and white/ light blue for the Highland.

F: LIBYA, 1912–33

F1: *Muntaz*, 6th Native Battalion; Cyrenaica, 1916
The first Libyan *ascari* recruited in 1912 were dressed in simple semi-regular clothing. Instead of the *tarbusc*, the traditional Libyan headdress was this lower red *tachia* soft cap with a medium blue tassel, worn over a white skull cap. A long white blouse was worn over loose white trousers, with coloured waist-sashes. During the last months of 1912, however, their dress was 'regularised' as illustrated here. The knee-length blouse became more regular in cut, and, where appropriate, displayed red points-up rank chevrons attached to the sleeves. Over it the *ascari* wore a waistcoat like that of the Somali troops (see Plate C1), in battalion colours. That of the 6th Bn was yellow, with white edging and medium blue embroidery, worn with a waist-sash striped yellow/ medium blue. The trousers were worn with khaki puttees, and these distinctive sandals with a high tongue. From 1913 a khaki version of the universal blouse, with two breast pockets, began to be produced. This became increasingly popular, and from 1920 it was the usual campaign dress (though the white blouse with coloured waistcoat continued to be worn on parade). The new

regulations of 1928 would introduce a completely different service uniform (see Plate G2), but the khaki blouse continued to be worn on campaign (and was modified in 1937 to become shorter). Libyan artillerymen were dressed like the infantry, with the usual yellow branch colour; they could be distinguished by entirely yellow waist-sashes, and by waistcoats that were black with yellow embroidery for Tripolitanian units, and in reversed colours for Cyrenaican gunners.

F2: *Savaro*, 1st Squadron; Tripolitania, 1926
Until 1926 the *Savari* had only a very practical campaign uniform, consisting of the red *tachia* wrapped with a coloured scarf like a turban; a khaki jacket with fold-down collar and two chest pockets; a waist-sash; khaki trousers, and brown leather sandals. The headgear-scarf and the waist-sash were in distinctive unit colours. In 1926 the white parade dress reconstructed here was introduced, including this heavily embroidered waistcoat in squadron colours, and brown leather knee-gaiters. The 1928 dress regulations would introduce a new campaign uniform, with khaki jacket and trousers similar to those worn by the infantry (see Plate G2).

In the gendarmerie the foot *zaptiè* were dressed like the infantry, and the mounted ones like the *savari*, but both with common distinctions of their service. Their red *tachia* had a white-metal flaming-grenade badge; the jacket collar was red, with two silver-braid stripes; and their waist-sash was red. The mounted *zaptiè* of the governor's bodyguard in Tripoli added a red waistcoat with white embroidery including flaming-grenade motifs, and on parade they wore a magnificent red *burnous* cloak broadly similar in shape to that of figure F3.

China, 1900: two soldiers – literally, mounted infantrymen, on sturdy local Manchurian ponies – of the *Plotone Esploratori a Cavallo dell'Estremo Oriente*. See under Plate H1 for this temporary uniform.

F3: Spahis, 1st Group; Tripolitania, 1929

These 'semi-regular' light cavalry received their first regular uniform, as illustrated here, only in 1924. Copied from the traditional dress of the Libyan *bedouin,* it was based on the single long, loose white garment known as a *parasia.* This was worn together with a *smala* hood, under which the red *tachia* is barely visible. Over it this rider wears a very capacious dark blue *burnous* cloak decorated with crimson edging and embroidery, with the hood thrown back over his shoulders. The *Spahi* used Arab horse furniture, while the *Savari* were equipped with Italian cavalry harness. The carbine is the ubiquitous M1891 *moschetto da cavalleria.*

G: LIBYA, 1934–42

G1: Muntaz, 7th Native Battalion, 1940

This reconstructs the new khaki uniform introduced by the 1928 dress regulations, which was still in use during World War II. The tucked-in jacket has a standing collar with the Italian Army's star badges, shoulder straps, and box-pleated breast pockets; the red rank chevrons have now been reduced in size. As an alternative to this, Libyan infantrymen could wear the khaki blouse, which had been introduced in 1913 and shortened in 1937; known as the *camiciotto,* this had two pockets and a buttoning fly part-way down the chest. Since the early 1920s the *tachia* had begun to display crowned brass arm-of-service badges, that of the infantry showing crossed bugle-horns and rifles. The cap-tassel was now always blue. Two-coloured waist-sashes – here, in the 7th Bn's red and medium blue – continued to differentiate units. The rifle is the standard 6.5mm M1891 Carcano. (For one table of colonial infantry unit waist-sash colours in 1940, see MAA 349, *The Italian Army 1940–45 (2): Africa 1940–43;* however, this subject is still a matter of some debate between researchers.)

G2: Bulukbasci, Meharisti, 1st Saharan Group, 1935

The early camel troops had received a uniform similar to that of Plate F1, with a dark blue waistcoat embroidered in red, and a red waist-sash. Very soon, however, a new campaign dress based on traditional *bedouin* costume came into use. This comprised three main elements: a turban, a light *suria* blouse and loose *sirual* trousers (as with all Arabic terms, this is variously transcribed in European texts, as *saroual, serwal*, etc.). All these were khaki in colour, and both the blouse and the trousers had two pockets. Over time, waist-sashes in distinctive unit colours began to appear, and a four-pocket khaki jacket might be worn over the blouse. From 1928-29 this new uniform also started to be produced in the white version illustrated; this was worn mainly for parade dress, together with this extra-long scarf in the same unit colours as the waist-sash (here, red/ black), worn over the shoulders and crossed at the front. With the adoption of the new 'bedouin' uniform, in khaki or white, the camel units adopted the same black rank brassards looped onto the sleeves as worn by the Eritrean colonial units. During World War II it was not uncommon to see a *meharista* wearing khaki turban and jacket with a white *suria* and *sirual.* Since they were mostly tasked with mounted-infantry duties, the Libyan camel troops were usually armed with the M1891 infantry rifle.

G3: Ascaro, Paratroop Training Battalion 'Air Infantry', 1938–39

Demonstrating his exit leap to the sceptical infantryman is a soldier of Italy's first parachute unit. In 1938, the 300 Libyan volunteers of the *Battaglione Allievi Paracadutisti 'Fanteria dell'Aria'* were uniformed in the khaki M1937 *camiciotto* blouse, with a blue/white striped waist-sash, and old-style rank-and-service brassards. A few months before the outbreak of World War II in 1939, the so-called *'Ascari del Cielo'* received this new khaki jump-suit with four zipped front pockets. Silver stars were worn on the fold-down collar and a striking (if unofficial) red-and-blue parachute qualification badge on the left breast, and the unit sash was retained. The overall was worn with a leather *elmetto da paracadutista,* and the personal weapon was the M1891 Carcano cavalry carbine. The original jump training was carried out with Salvator D37 parachutes, but their eccentrically designed harness led to 100-plus injuries and 20 fatalities in two months, so jumping was discontinued until the improved D39 and similar D40 became available.

H: LOCALLY-RAISED & EXPEDITIONARY UNITS, 1900–20

While none of these random overseas expeditions was truly 'colonial', nor did they involve colonial units, we include brief mention of them here purely out of interest.

H1: Trooper, Plotone Esploratori a Cavallo dell'Estremo Oriente; China, 1900

The expeditionary corps sent to take part in the 'eight-nation alliance' against the Boxer Rebellion in northern China in 1900 comprised three composite units, each with four companies: a naval landing battalion, and a battalion each of line infantry and *Bersaglieri.* These initially wore the M1887 khaki uniform issued to the *Cacciatori d'Africa* in 1889, but with the coming of winter this was replaced with standard dark blue Italian metropolitan dress. A small cavalry reconnaissance platoon, improvised in-country from suitable line and light infantrymen, wore the peculiar temporary dress reconstructed here. The black fur light-cavalry 'busby' had a red crown, a black feather rising from a red pompon, and a green tassel. The dark blue cape with a fold-down collar was worn over the dark blue uniform, of which only the trousers with a red side-stripe are visible here. The soldiers were mounted on small Manchurian ponies, and armed with M1891 cavalry carbines.

The rankers of the *Battaglione Italiano in Cina,* partly detached from the 'San Marco' Naval Inf Regt to garrison the Tienstsin Concession from 1924, used two different uniforms. These were cut like the contemporary dress of Italian Navy sailors, but in two alternate colours: *grigioverde* for the single naval infantry company, and blue for the two companies of sailors. Their officers wore the same uniforms as their Army or Navy equivalents.

H2: Private, 'Black Battalion', Legione Redenta di Siberia; Tientsin, 1919

This little-known two-battalion 'redeemed legion' was organized in Tientsin during summer 1918, from among some 2,500 ethnic northern Italians who had been serving in the Austro-Hungarian Army. Captured in Russia, when released they had made their way across Siberia to reach the Italian concession in China. They were uniformed almost entirely with surplus clothing provided by the Imperial Japanese Army, which was then allied to the Entente powers. This soldier's only Italian item is the *cappello alpino* of the mountain troops, with raven feather and national cockade. Otherwise he wears Japanese M1911 khaki uniform with black patches on the collar and shoulders; the other battalion

Basic jacket details

Colony	Branch	Issue	Colour	Cut	Collar	Shldr straps	Pkts	Front pleats
Eritrea	inf & arty	1890	white	short	stand			
Eritrea	inf & arty & zaptiè	1901	khaki	long	stand	yes	4	yes
Eritrea	inf & arty	1904	white	short	stand		2	
Eritrea	inf & arty	1908	khaki	long	stand	yes	4	
Eritrea	inf & arty & zaptiè	1928	khaki	long	stand	yes	4	
Eritrea	cavalry	1908	khaki & white	long	stand	yes	4	yes
Eritrea	cavalry	1928	khaki & white	long	stand	yes	4	
Eritrea	zaptiè	1887	white	short	stand	yes		yes
Eritrea	zaptiè	1908	khaki	short	stand	no	2	
Eritrea	armed bands	1931	khaki	long	stand	yes	4	
Somalia	inf & arty	1913	khaki & white	long	folded	yes	2	
Somalia	inf & arty	1928	khaki & white	long	stand	yes	4	
Somalia	zaptiè	1922	khaki	long	folded	yes	2	
Somalia	zaptiè	1928	white	long	stand	yes		
Libya	inf & arty & zaptiè	1913	khaki	long	stand	yes	2	
Libya	inf & arty & zaptiè	1928	khaki	long	stand	yes	4	
Libya	inf & arty & zaptiè	1937	khaki	short	stand	yes	2	
Libya	Savari	1913	khaki	short	folded	yes	2	
Libya	Savari	1928	khaki	long	stand	yes	4	

Note: The numbering of figures on any one plate does not follow their position on the page, but the chronological development of uniforms.

wore these in red. His equipment is also Japanese, and he carries an Arisaka Type 38 rifle. The 'redeemed legion' later linked up with a token Italian intervention force sent to support the 'Whites' in the Russian Civil War; this saw very little action, and returned to Italy in February 1920.

H3: *Appuntato, Carabinieri Reali*; Adalya, Anatolia, 1920
During 1919, after the collapse of the Ottoman Empire, Greece received encouragement from the Entente powers for an invasion of Turkish Anatolia, which was resisted by Turkish Nationalist troops led by Mustafa Kemal Pasha (the future Ataturk).[5] When the Greek Army made considerable advances into central Anatolia, Italy also attempted to acquire some territory on the south-west coast. Rome sent an expeditionary force to occupy the port of Adalya (modern Antalya) and an area inland and west of it; this provoked furious objections from Athens, and, apart from the port itself (handed back to Turkey in 1923), all the occupied area was ceded to the Greeks after a matter of months. The Italian troops committed were a strong mixed brigade of line infantry and *Bersaglieri* with supporting cavalry, artillery and engineer elements, plus a platoon of *Carabinieri*. These wore the standard M1909 *grigioverde* uniform, with riding breeches but puttees for dismounted duty. They were distinguishable most immediately by their *lucerna* bicorne hat (here with a canvas cover stencilled with the corps badge), but also by the silver-braid patches on their black collars. Leather equipment was polished black; the weapons are a holstered revolver on the left hip, and the M1891 cavalry carbine.

---

5   See MAA 501, *Armies of the Greek-Turkish War 1919–22.*

INDEX

Page numbers in bold refer to illustrations and their captions.